E/ESCWA/CL2.GPID/2026/2

Economic and Social Commission for Western Asia

The Hidden Sector:
Just Transitions to the Formal Economy

UNITED NATIONS
Beirut

United Nations publication issued by ESCWA, United Nations House, Riad El Solh Square,
P.O. Box: 11-8575, Beirut, Lebanon.

Website: www.unescwa.org.

UNITED NATIONS PUBLICATION
E/ESCWA/CL2.GPID/2026/2
PRINT ISBN: 9789211577440
PDF ISBN: 9789211546842
Sales no: E.26.II.L.3
2500651E

Acknowledgements

The present publication was produced by the United Nations Economic and Social Commission for Western Asia (ESCWA) under the supervision and guidance of the Executive Secretary.

Report team

Oussama Safa, Chief, Social Justice Section, Gender Justice, Population and Inclusive Development Cluster, authored this report and led a core team of co-authors from the Social Justice Section comprising Angela Samara, Researcher in Social Development Issues, and Zahraa Barakat, Research Assistant in Economics.

Key messages

Informality is systemic, not marginal. Nearly **72 per cent of workers in the Arab region are in informal employment,** spanning all ages and job types. Over 90 per cent of young people and older persons are informally employed, revealing failures in both labour market entry and retirement security.

Women bear the heaviest burden. In some countries, nearly **half of women in informal work are unpaid, without rights or autonomy.**

Education does not guarantee decent work. A severe skills-labour market mismatch is evidenced by **40.7 per cent of university graduates in the region remaining in informal employment,** more than double the global average.

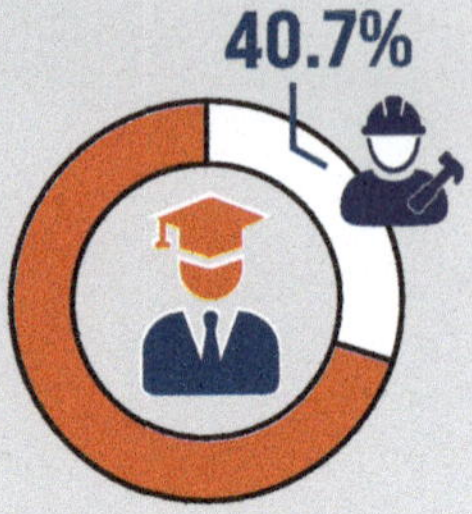

Financial exclusion locks out informal workers.
Lack of bank accounts, collateral and credit history makes it nearly impossible for informal actors to access loans and investment.

Climate change and conflict deepen informality. Extreme climate events and conflict-related shocks, which destroy crops, disrupt supply chains, and wipe out fragile incomes, force many to rely on informal coping strategies. Without social protection, these groups lose livelihoods overnight and face heightened vulnerability.

Costs and bureaucracy deter formalization. For many informal actors, licensing, taxes and complex procedures outweigh benefits. Formalization risks **appear burdensome rather than empowering.**

One-size-fits-all approaches do not work. **Targeted sectoral policies are needed to create real incentives for workers and businesses** to transition to formality, as the largest share of informal employment is found in agriculture, construction, street vending and small-scale manufacturing, where wages are lower, job security is minimal, and social protections are almost non-existent.

Secure and inclusive housing is central to social and economic inclusion. Informality in both employment and shelter continues to reinforce cycles of exclusion. Tackling informal urban settlements through integrated and inclusive housing policies is essential to reducing inequality.

Digital tools are a game-changer. Digital platforms are simplifying registration, tax payments, and access to services. **E-formalization makes the transition simpler, cheaper and more attractive.**

Executive summary

While the informal economy in the Arab region provides livelihoods for millions, particularly marginalized populations including women, young people and displaced individuals, informality represents economic instability, a lack of social protection, and limited access to financial services. This report examines the challenges, trends and policy frameworks required for a just transition from informality to formality in the Arab region.

Informal employment rates in the Arab region between 2014 and 2024 are at 71.8 per cent, exceeding the global average of 60 per cent. Informal employment is characterized by demographic disparities and vulnerabilities and accounts for an estimated 44.9 million workers. Marginalized groups, particularly young people, 90 per cent of whom are in informal employment, and older persons, face significant challenges due to limited job opportunities and inadequate pension systems. Women are disproportionately affected, as they are overrepresented in low-wage, insecure jobs, such as home-based enterprises and unregistered domestic work. Despite good rates of higher educational attainment, 40.7 per cent of university graduates remain in informal employment, more than double the global average, highlighting a severe skills mismatch and significant barriers to formal employment.

Structural economic limitations, high unemployment, weak enforcement of labour laws, and burdensome bureaucratic requirements for formalization contribute to the high informality rates. Informality persists across agriculture, construction, domestic work and emerging digital economies. The absence of social protection mechanisms for informal workers exacerbates poverty and economic vulnerability, especially in times of crisis. Successful global and regional initiatives, including tax incentives, cooperative models and social solidarity economies, offer lessons for transitioning to formality.

The present report emphasizes the need for holistic and inclusive policies that recognize the socioeconomic realities of informal workers. A just transition to formality entails fostering sustainable, equitable economic structures that uphold labour rights, enhance productivity, and ensure long-term stability.

Key recommendations include the need for regulatory reforms which streamline registration and licensing processes, reduce bureaucratic barriers, and incentivize businesses to formalize. Social protection systems must be expanded, and financial inclusion and access to credit need to be enhanced. The mismatch between education systems and labour market must be addressed to reduce informality among young job seekers. Finally, partnerships between Governments, private sector actors and civil society must be strengthened to facilitate sustainable formalization pathways.

Contents

Acknowledgements 3

Key messages 4

Executive summary 7

Introduction and overview 10

1. Scope, objectives and methodology 12

2. What defines an informal economy 13

3. Characteristics, drivers and statistical trends of the informal economy in the Arab region 15

4. Challenges and barriers to transitioning to a formal economy in the Arab region 23

5. Forecasting informal employment and evaluating policy interventions: The case of Egypt 29
   - A. Model specification 30
   - B. Results and findings 31
   - C. Policy scenario: tax intervention 32

6. Global and regional examples of just transitions 34
   - A In the Arab region 34
   - B. In Africa 36
   - C. In Latin America 37
   - D. In Asia 38
   - E. Leveraging technology for just transitions 40
   - F. Emerging role of social solidarity structures in assuring just transitions 41

7. Concluding observations and practical policy recommendations for just transitions 43
   - A. Concluding observations 43
   - B. Suggested practical solutions for Governments 44

Annex. Evolution of the International Conference of Labour Statisticians Standards 48

Endnotes 50

List of tables

Table 1. Wage distribution by sector: formal vs. informal employees (Local currency) 21
Table 2. Coefficients and significance of exogenous variables 32
Table 3. Summary of selected regional and global interventions that encourage just transitions 39

List of figures

Figure 1. Types of informal employment 14
Figure 2. Informal employment rates in the Arab region (2014-2024) by age group, latest available year per country 16
Figure 3. Informal employment rate (15+), by country, sex and latest available year 17
Figure 4. Informal employment rate, by education level 18
Figure 5. Share of informal employment in total employment by country, including agriculture 19
Figure 6. Share of informal employment in total employment by country, excluding agriculture 19
Figure 7. Percentage of informal workers by employment status, by country, sex and latest available year 20
Figure 8. Median sales per worker 22
Figure 9. Median profits per worker 22
Figure 10. Perceived benefits of business registration across countries 27
Figure 11. Informal employment rate 2008-2030 32
Figure 12. Forecasts of informal employment rate, 2024-2030 - baseline scenario compared to policy scenario 34
Figure A.1 Major milestones of ICLS resolutions on standards for measuring informality 48

List of boxes

Box 1. Waste collectors in Brazil 25
Box 2. Transitioning from informality to formality: the Tizwa project 35
Box 3. Law 2125 in Colombia 36
Box 4. Other solidarity-based interventions 41
Box 5. A suggested model for tax incentives 45

Introduction and overview

The informal sector is significant across much of the Arab region, encompassing a considerable percentage of employment and economic activity. This constitutes a critical challenge for economies in the Arab region, where informal employment accounts for nearly 71.8 per cent of the labour market, undermining trust in public institutions and perpetuating inequality, particularly among women and young people. Gender disparities are apparent, with 73.5 per cent of employed men compared to 63.5 per cent of employed women engaged in the informal employment.

Informality has become the leading source of livelihood for many vulnerable segments of society, cutting across urban and rural settings, sex, disability, age, migration and displacement status, thus affecting millions of individuals who lack access to social protection, labour rights and economic security. These same groups are also most affected by increasing housing costs, as they are unable to access formal housing markets or secure home ownership. In 2024, over 35 per cent of young people under the age of 25 years in the Comoros, Iraq, Jordan and Yemen faced tenure insecurity in housing.[1] When these groups lose their jobs or experience sharp income losses due to external shocks, they become highly vulnerable, risking falling even further behind, as seen during the COVID-19 pandemic.

Limited job opportunities, low economic productivity and high unemployment rates have resulted in the expansion of informality. Many countries in the Arab region experience varying unemployment rates, ranging from as low as 0.13 per cent in Qatar (2022) to as high as 24 per cent in the occupied Palestinian territory (2022).[2] Averaging 10.2 per cent (2024),[3] unemployment in the Arab region is particularly high among young people (25.2 per cent) and women (18.3 per cent).[4] The Arab region needs to create more than 33 million jobs to reduce unemployment by 5 per cent by 2030;[5] for young women, employment needs to increase sixfold for gender equity to be achieved.
[6] The region's young population intensifies the pressure on already stressed formal labour markets, which cannot meet the increasing demands for jobs, compelling many young people to swell the ranks of the informal sector.

The challenges associated with informality extend beyond economic factors to significant social implications, as informal workers struggle with heightened risks of poverty, job insecurity and unpredictable income. This marginalization excludes them from decision-making processes, deepening their social and economic vulnerabilities.[7]

The COVID-19 pandemic, during which 27 million informal workers (89 per cent of those informally employed)[8] were significantly impacted, further exposed the vulnerabilities of informal workers, emphasizing the need for Governments to integrate decent employment, social protection and sustainable development into national development plans. People resort to informal employment for a variety of reasons, primarily as a response to the breakdown of the social contract, whereby their basic needs and rights are unmet. A strengthened social contract in the Arab region goes hand in hand with just transitions, as it relies on building trust in State institutions, inclusive governance and equitable labour policies that promote sustainable development and economic mobility.

Informal workers such as agricultural workers, small-scale informal enterprises, and street vendors are disproportionately affected by the impacts of extreme climate events, which force them to migrate or lose their livelihoods and expose them to significant risks due to a lack of social protection during climate-related disasters. In conflict-affected countries, informal economic activities increase and become a coping mechanism for various segments of the population affected by conflict and displacement, leaving them further behind.

In 2015, the International Labour Organization (ILO) adopted Recommendation 204, emphasizing the need to transition from an informal to a formal economy and providing guidance for Governments on the formalization process. While many countries have developed strategies or adopted policies and measures to facilitate this transition, formalization remains a complex and long-term process that often necessitates cross-cutting interventions at the legal, regulatory, labour market, tax and productivity levels.

The path to formality promotes inclusive development and empowers vulnerable groups by reinforcing the rule of law and addressing economic vulnerabilities. It can expand the tax base, allowing Governments to collect more revenue and provide more services in exchange.[9]

1. Scope, objectives and methodology

This report briefly describes the main characteristics, drivers and trends of the informal economy in the Arab region. It portrays the composition and distribution of informal employment by sector, age, sex and employment status, revealing country-level variations. It discusses the main challenges and barriers to transitioning to a formal economy in the Arab region, presenting concrete examples of experiences from around the globe of the successful adoption of measures and implementation of targeted interventions to ensure formalization.

The report relies on quantitative research approaches to provide robust and reliable analysis. It utilizes available data from ILOSTAT and labour force surveys, based on which the necessary calculations were undertaken by the United Nations Economic and Social Commission for Western Asia (ESCWA). To depict the policy interventions relevant for reducing informal employment by 2030, using the example of Egypt, the study applies an autoregressive integrated moving average with exogenous factors (ARIMAX) time series model, which analyses and forecasts the impact of selected exogenous factors on the informal employment rate to understand the incentives for formalization. We also rely on desk research and literature review to identify barriers and challenges to formalization, and best practices for a just transition. The paper concludes with recommended action and practical solutions for Governments and for ESCWA to facilitate a just transition to a formal economy in the Arab region.

2. What defines an informal economy

Over the past 30 years, the International Conference of Labour Statisticians (ICLS) has refined standards for measuring informality, adapting to evolving labour markets and expanding the concept of work beyond formal employment. These updates influence the scope and size of the informal sector, ensuring labour statistics remain relevant for policy development and global comparability.[10]

According to ILO Recommendation 204, the informal economy encompasses all economic activities, excluding illicit activities, conducted by workers and economic units that are either not covered or insufficiently covered by formal arrangements, whether in law or in practice. Informal workers are essentially those who are not protected by national labour legislation, do not pay income tax, and are not entitled to social protection or other employment benefits. Accordingly, three groups of informal workers are identified as: employee, employer or own-account worker, and contributing family worker.[11]

Employees are considered informally employed if their employer does not contribute to social security on their behalf, which means they are not entitled to benefits such as pensions, unemployment insurance or health coverage; or if they do not receive employment benefits such as paid annual or sick leave.

Employers include those with hired workers or own-account workers who do not have hired workers. These positions are considered informal if they are unregistered, lack formal bookkeeping, and usually do not comply with labour laws or tax regulations.

When informal employers hire others, they assume both managerial and operational roles but do so without the protection and obligations of formal businesses. Own-account workers run independent self-employed business operations.[12]

Contributing family workers are always classified as informally employed, regardless of the sector in which they work. They are also known as unpaid family workers as they primarily work in a family-owned business without direct pay. They are informally employed regardless of whether the family business operates in the formal or informal sector. Their work is often characterized by a lack of formal contracts, and they are not entitled to social security benefits or labour regulation benefits such as paid leave. This form of informal employment is prevalent in agriculture, retail, craftwork and home-based industries.[13]

Figure 1. Types of informal employment

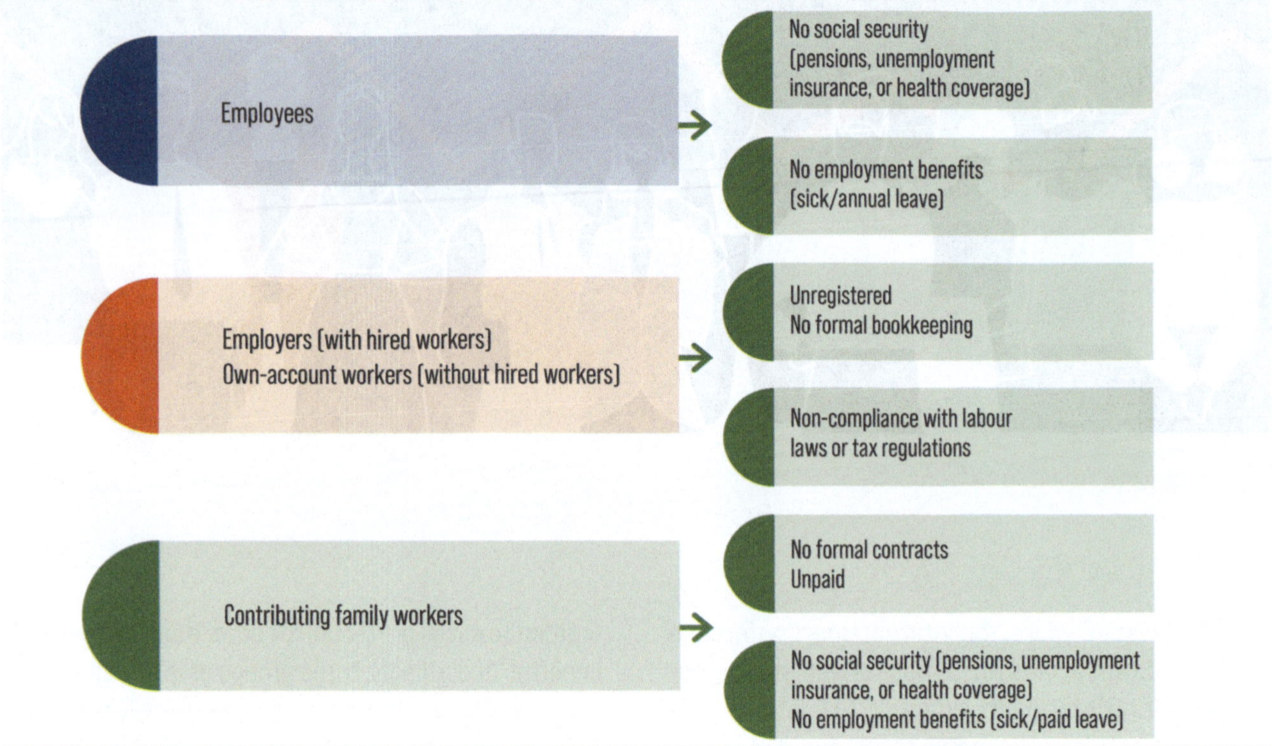

Source: Developed by the authors based on definitions provided by ILO.

The latest 21st ICLS, held in 2023, acknowledged new employment modalities, particularly within the gig economy[14] and digital platforms, such as Uber drivers, food delivery couriers, and freelancers on online platforms. It recognized that these types of labour often obscure the distinction between self-employment and wage employment, creating new challenges in assessing employment relationships and safeguarding workers' rights.[15]

In some non-standard forms of employment, the employer-employee relationship is legally recognized but is not governed by any form of protection, continuity or job security. Shock-responsive employment has become a pressing challenge, especially post-COVID-19, as many people resorted to informal employment due to lockdowns and have been unable to return to formal arrangements. The emergence of the digital economy, with big data, remote work and increasing reliance on artificial intelligence, will undoubtedly reshape both the formal and informal sectors in the years ahead.

3. Characteristics, drivers and statistical trends of the informal economy in the Arab region

High informal employment rates in the Arab region,[16] averaging 71.8 per cent[17] between 2014 and 2024 (figure 2) and accounting for an estimated 44.9 million individuals,[18] are the result of deep-rooted structural challenges within labour markets. This figure significantly exceeds the global average of 60 per cent,[19] highlighting the existence of significant barriers to formalization across the region. The distribution of informal employment across demographic groups reveals critical vulnerabilities, particularly among young people (aged 15–24 years) and older persons (65+ years), which exhibit the highest rates at around 90 per cent. For young people, this reflects systemic shortcomings in the transition from education to formal employment, indicating a mismatch between educational outcomes and labour market needs. For older persons, limited or non-existent pension systems compel them to rely on informal and often insecure jobs, revealing deficiencies in social protection policies. Even among workers aged between 25–54 years and 55–64 years, high informal employment rates of 68 per cent and 65.5 per cent, respectively, demonstrate the structural prevalence of informality across the population, indicating inadequate mechanisms for formal job creation and workforce integration.

Figure 2. Informal employment rates in the Arab region (2014-2024) by age group, latest available year per country (Percentage)

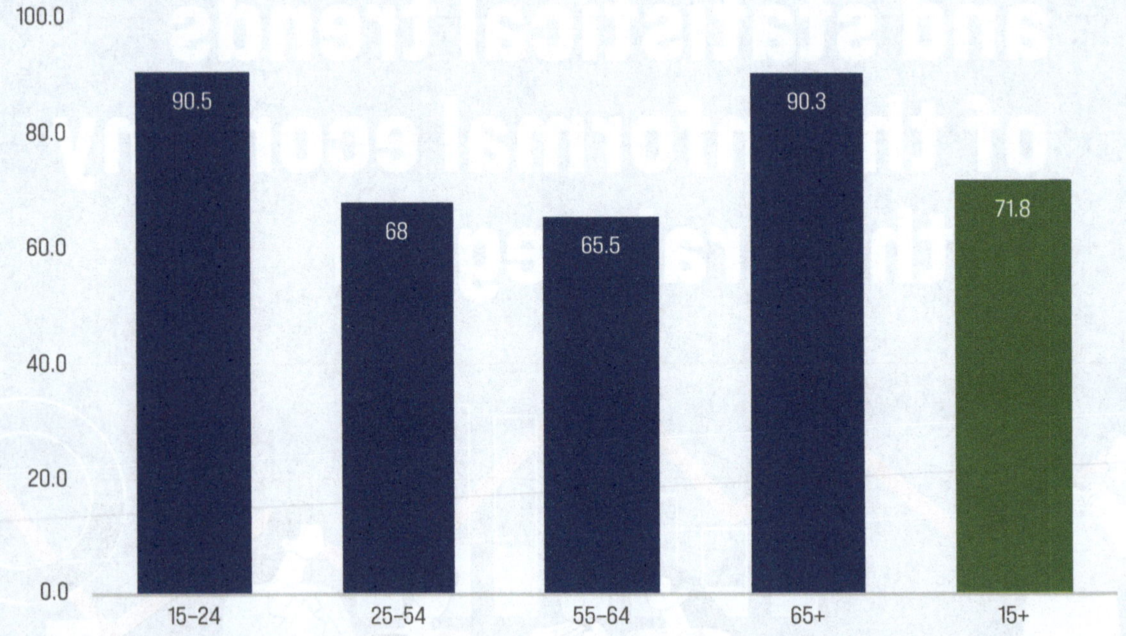

Source: ESCWA calculation based on ILOSTAT. The regional average of informal employment rates is calculated based on the latest available data for each country. The years of the most recent data vary across countries: the Comoros (2021), Djibouti (2017), Egypt (2023), Iraq (2021), Jordan (2023), Lebanon (2019), Mauritania (2019), occupied Palestinian territory (2024), the Sudan (2022), Somalia (2019), Tunisia (2019) and Yemen (2014). The Arab region average (green) covers the period from 2014-2024.

Country-level variations (figure 3) further accentuate the uneven progress in addressing informality. Countries such as the Sudan (94.4 per cent), Mauritania (89.4 per cent), the Comoros (88.8 per cent) and Somalia (82.5 per cent) exhibit high rates of informal employment. These rates are indicative of weak institutional frameworks, limited economic diversification, and inadequate enforcement of labour regulations. In contrast, the comparatively lower rate of 36.9 per cent in Tunisia is the result of a more robust policy environment and advancements towards formalization, despite ongoing challenges. These discrepancies emphasize the necessity for tailored interventions and a career-cycle approach to reduce informality.

Gender disparities within informal employment reveal deep inequalities and systemic challenges faced by women. In the Comoros, Djibouti, Mauritania and Somalia, women consistently exhibit higher rates of informal employment than men, often occupying less secure and lower-paid roles. For instance, in the Comoros, 91.6 per cent of employed women are engaged in informal employment compared to 86.7 per cent of employed men. In Djibouti, the disparity is even more pronounced, with 64.9 per cent of women informally employed compared to 45.7 per cent of men. These trends indicate structural barriers, such as limited access to formal job opportunities, discriminatory practices, and the concentration of women in sectors with low formalization rates. The overrepresentation of women in informal employment also reflects societal norms and caregiving responsibilities, which constrain their labour market participation and mobility.

Figure 3. Informal employment rate (15+), by country, sex and latest available year (Percentage)

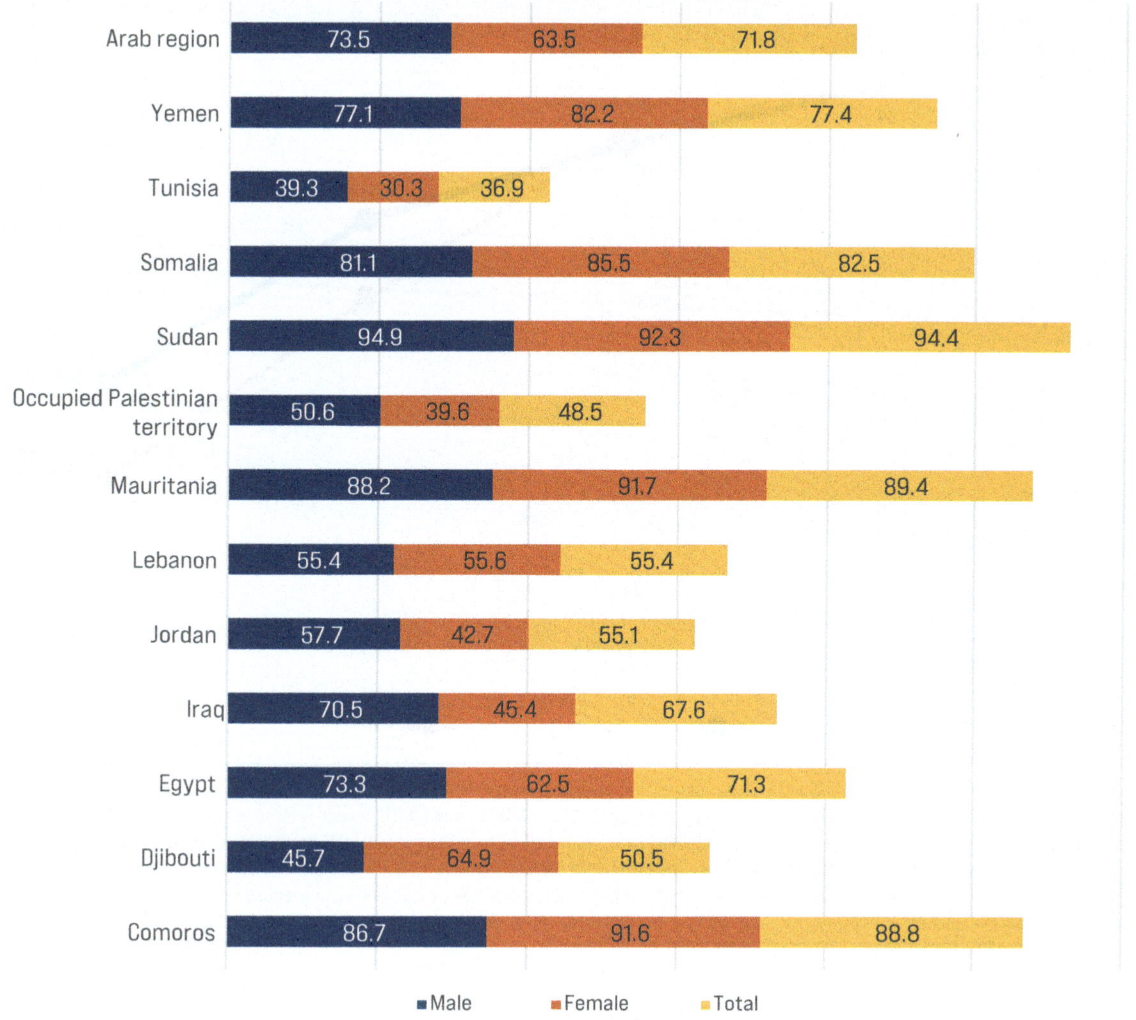

Source: ESCWA calculation based on ILOSTAT. The regional average of informal employment rates is calculated based on the latest available data among 12 countries. The years of the most recent data vary across countries: the Comoros (2021), Djibouti (2017), Egypt (2023), Iraq (2021), Jordan (2023), Lebanon (2019), Mauritania (2019), occupied Palestinian territory (2024), the Sudan (2022), Somalia (2019), Tunisia (2019) and Yemen (2014). Arab region average covers the period from 2014-2024.

While global trends demonstrate that higher education significantly decreases informal employment, the Arab region presents a paradox (figure 4). Among individuals with no education, informal employment is extremely high in both the Arab region and globally, at 94 per cent. At the primary education level, informality in the region (83.2 per cent) remains close to the global trend (85.9 per cent). However, as educational attainment rises, the gap widens. Informality among those with secondary education reaches 70 per cent in the Arab region, far exceeding the global average of 56 per cent. Most strikingly, 40.7 per cent of tertiary-educated individuals in the region are in informal employment, almost double the global rate of 23.9 per cent. There is an urgent need to tackle informality among educated workers by creating decent jobs and addressing barriers to formal employment, such as the skills mismatch, the quality of education systems and constraints to market entry.

Figure 4. Informal employment rate, by education level (Percentage)

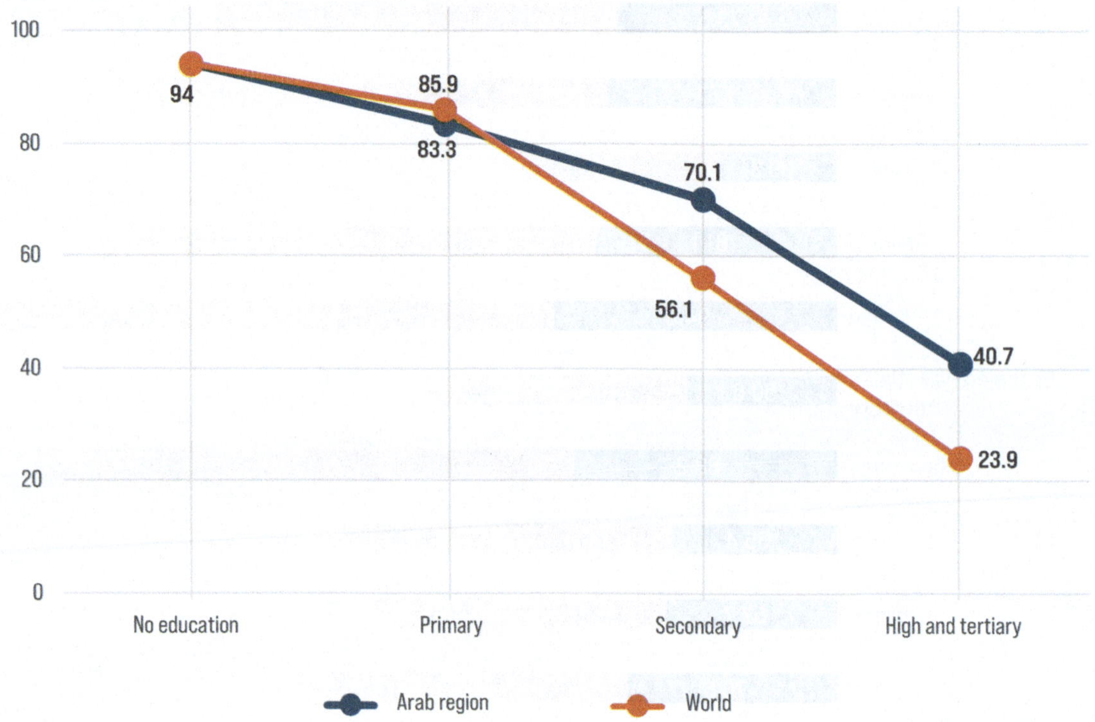

Source: ESCWA calculation based on data from the ILO database. The regional average of informal employment rates is calculated based on data from the latest available year for each country: the Comoros (2021), Djibouti (2017), Egypt (2023), Iraq (2021), Jordan (2023), Lebanon (2019), Mauritania (2019), occupied Palestinian territory (2024), the Sudan (2022), Somalia (2019), Tunisia (2019) and Yemen (2014). The education classification used in this analysis is as follows: no education refers to no schooling. Primary education covers early childhood education and primary education. Secondary education encompasses lower secondary education and upper secondary education. High and tertiary education includes post-secondary non-tertiary education, short-cycle tertiary education, bachelor's or equivalent level, master's or equivalent level, and doctoral or equivalent level.

Barriers to transitioning to a formal economy can be broadly classified into financial, legal, regulatory, administrative, institutional, political, social and cultural categories. These barriers significantly deter or obstruct informal businesses from formalizing their operations. Many informal enterprises lack incentives to formalize, particularly when the direct financial benefits remain ambiguous or difficult to attain.

The composition of informal employment by sector and employment status (figure 5) offers significant insights into the dynamics of informality within the Arab region. Informal employment within the informal sector prevails across the majority of countries, with the Comoros demonstrating the highest share at 84.6 per cent, followed by Yemen at 68.5 per cent and the Syrian Arab Republic at 66 per cent. Nevertheless, in certain countries, informal employment within the formal sector constitutes a substantial proportion of total informal employment, particularly when agricultural employment is excluded; this is evident in Morocco (20.4 per cent) and the occupied Palestinian territory (34.2 per cent). This indicates that a considerable number of informal workers operate within formal enterprises yet remain outside the purview of labour regulations, social protections and taxation, thereby highlighting deficiencies in enforcement and compliance mechanisms.

Figure 5. Share of informal employment in total employment by country, including agriculture (Percentage)

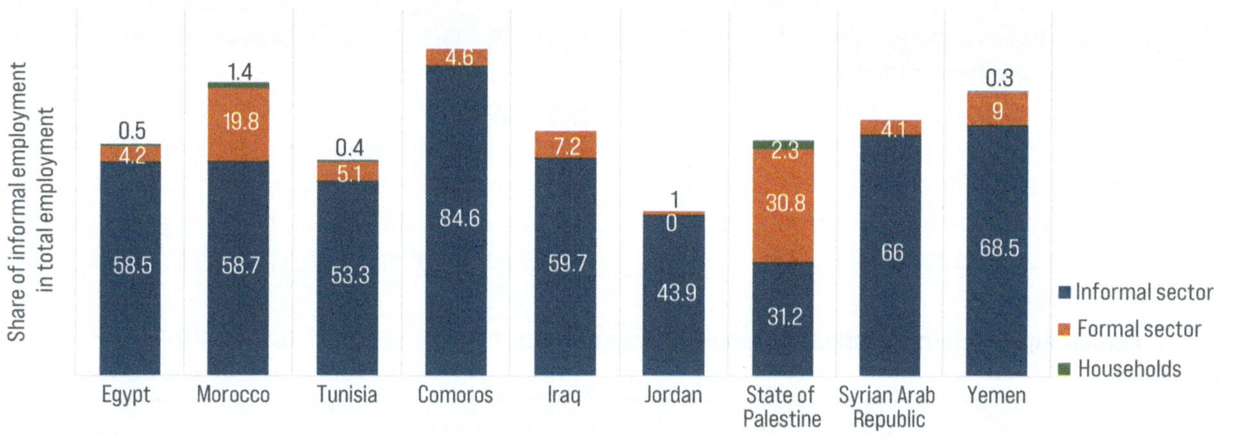

Source: Based on the method presented in ILO, Women and Men in the Informal Economy: A Statistical Picture, third edition, 2018, Appendix A.3. Calculations based on national labour force or similar household survey data. The total share of informal employment is divided into informal employment in the informal sector (informal economic units), in the formal sector (including government units and non-profit institutions) and in households (as paid domestic workers or own-account workers producing goods exclusively for own final use by their households).

Sector-specific dynamics play an important role in shaping informal employment rates. When the agricultural sector is excluded, the overall rate of informal employment decreases in most countries. However, this exclusion also increases the share of informal workers within formal enterprises, revealing that informality is not limited to agriculture alone. For Morocco and the State of Palestine, for example, removing agricultural workers results in a noticeable rise in informal employment inside formal-sector establishments. This indicates that many formal firms rely on informal labour arrangements, reflecting broader structural challenges to achieving full formalization across economic sectors. These patterns may also signal that firms and workers are aiming to avoid high tax burdens or substantial social security contributions, highlighting the need for comprehensive reforms that make formal employment more accessible and affordable.

Figure 6. Share of informal employment in total employment by country, excluding agriculture (Percentage)

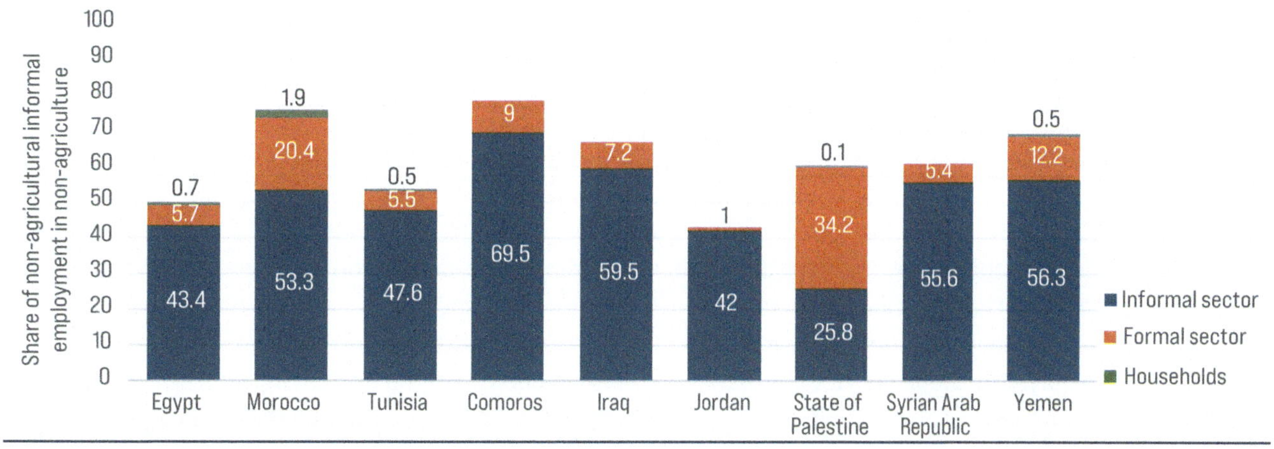

Source: Based on the method presented in ILO, Women and Men in the Informal Economy: A Statistical Picture, third edition, 2018, Appendix A.3. Calculations based on national labour force or similar household survey data. The total share of informal employment is divided into informal employment in the informal sector (informal economic units), in the formal sector (including government units and non-profit institutions) and in households (as paid domestic workers or own-account workers producing goods exclusively for own final use by their households).

Employees constitute the largest segment of informal workers in the region, accounting for 55.4 per cent of total informal employment (figure 7). Men are more likely to be informal employees (57.7 per cent) than women (41.1 per cent), reflecting gendered labour market dynamics, with some country variations. Women, however, are disproportionately represented among contributing family workers, one of the most vulnerable employment categories, with figures reaching 42.7 per cent in Egypt and 47.1 per cent in Yemen. These roles are characterized by low wages, limited rights and high dependency, further entrenching economic vulnerabilities among women. Employers constitute the smallest share of informal workers (9.1 per cent), with men significantly outnumbering women in this category, highlighting substantial gender disparities in entrepreneurship within the informal economy.

Figure 7. Percentage of informal workers by employment status, by country, sex and latest available year (Percentage)

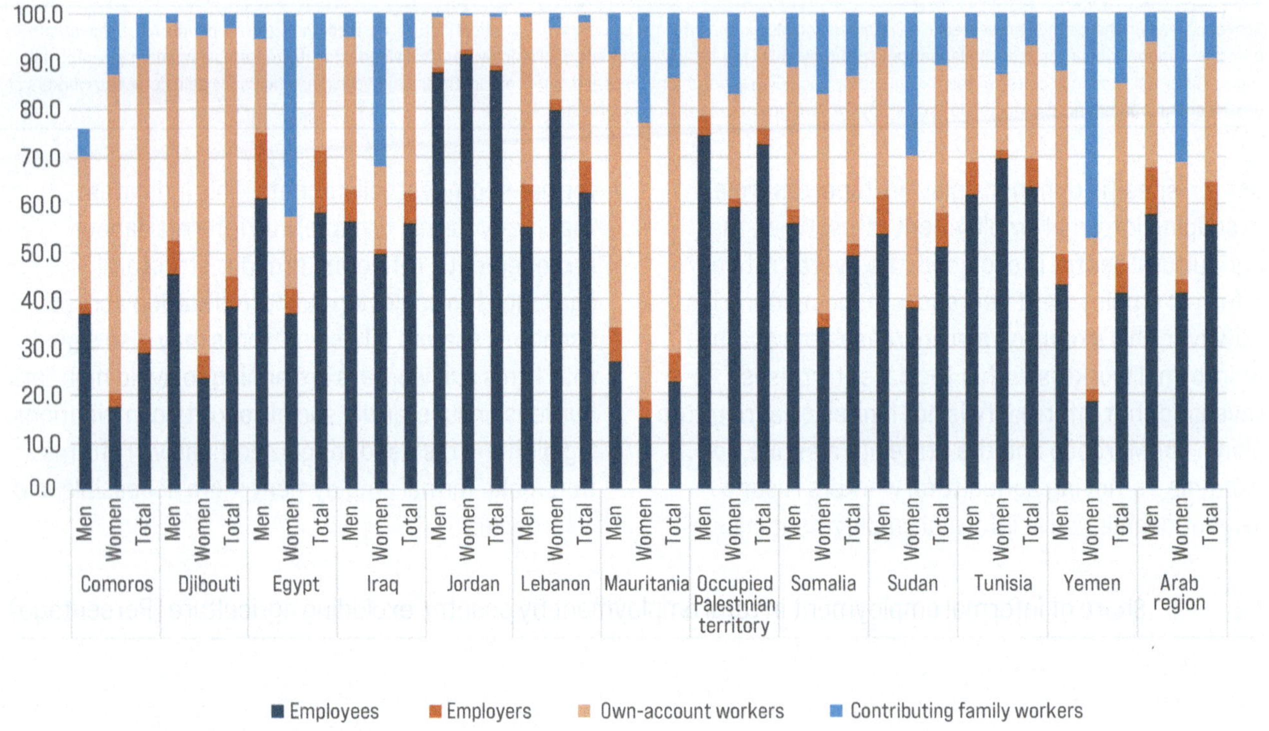

Source: ESCWA calculations based on ILOSTAT, latest available per country. The total percentage includes only employees, employers, own-account workers and contributing family workers. Workers not classified by employment status are excluded from the calculations. Arab region average covers the period from 2014-2022.

There are significant disparities in earnings between informal and formal workers (table 1), with formal employees generally receiving higher wages. A sector-specific analysis of wage distribution in Iraq and Egypt indicates that transitioning from informal to formal employment can yield substantial economic benefits, despite challenges present in sectors such as agriculture and construction. For instance, in Iraq, formal employees in the manufacturing sector earn more than twice the wages of their informal counterparts, with analogous patterns evident in trade and related services. In Egypt, although the wage disparities are smaller, formal employees still earn 16 per cent more in manufacturing and 7 per cent more in trade than those in informal employment. Conversely, in the construction sector, informal employees in Egypt earn slightly more than their formal counterparts, indicating potential disincentives to formalization, such as increased flexibility in informal arrangements. By contrast, the construction sector in Iraq exhibits higher wages for formal employees, thereby creating stronger incentives for formalization. The agricultural sector, however, demonstrates narrow wage differentials, which diminishes the attractiveness of formal employment, particularly in rural areas. The more pronounced wage gap between formal and informal employees in Iraq compared to Egypt reflects the disparities in their economic structures and labour market dynamics. In Iraq, formal employment often offers higher wages and benefits due to government expenditure bolstered by oil revenue, thereby creating a stark contrast with informal employment.

Table 1. Wage distribution by sector: formal vs. informal employees (Local currency)

	Egypt (Egyptian pounds)		Iraq (Iraqi dinars)	
	Formal	Informal	Formal	Informal
Agriculture	2,362	2,112	588,730	375,512
Manufacturing	2,635	2,272	798,387	440,416
Construction	2,901	3,113	954,540	402,276
Mining and quarrying, electricity, gas and water supply	2,870	2,465	783,667	467,374
Trade, transportation, accommodation, food, business and administrative services	2,768	2,580	736,655	454,544
Public administration, community, social and other services	2,434	2,039	909,037	605,750

Source: ESCWA calculations based on labour force surveys in Iraq 2021 and Egypt 2019.

The process of formalization represents a potentially transformative opportunity to enhance business productivity. Informal enterprises operate at significantly lower productivity levels relative to formal firms of comparable sizes. For instance, in Iraq, informal enterprises generate only 40 per cent of the median monthly sales of formal micro-enterprises ($344 versus $827) (figure 8). In Somalia, informal enterprises perform more favourably, achieving $125 in median sales per worker, which constitutes 63 per cent of the sales of their formal counterparts.

While the majority of informal businesses report generating a profit, their earnings are modest and limited (figure 8). Unlike sales per worker, which serves as an indicator of revenue generation, profit per worker reflects the residual earnings remaining after the deduction of costs. In Iraq, 63 per cent of firms indicate profitability, in contrast to 47 per cent in the Sudan and 36 per cent in Somalia.[20] However, as illustrated in figure 9, the average profit per worker remains low, with $200 per worker in Iraq and only $50 in both Somalia and the Sudan. This highlights the financial constraints faced by informal enterprises and the challenges to achieving sustainable profitability.

Figure 8. Median sales per worker (Dollars, last month)

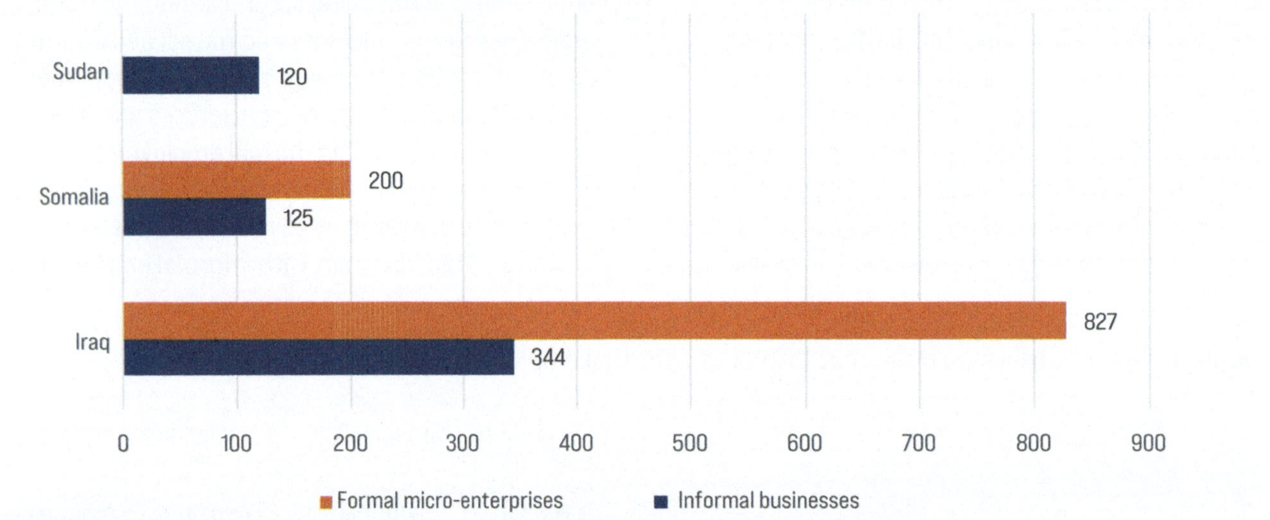

Source: ESCWA calculations based on informal enterprises survey and micro enterprises surveys retrieved from the World Bank. No micro enterprises survey was conducted in the Sudan.

The high prevalence of informal employment among the educated reflects structural deficiencies in the labour market and education systems. To unlock the potential of the region's educated workforce and foster inclusive economic development, effective skills-education matching programmes, fair wage policies and effective enforcement mechanisms should be priorities.

Figure 9. Median profits per worker (Dollars, last month)

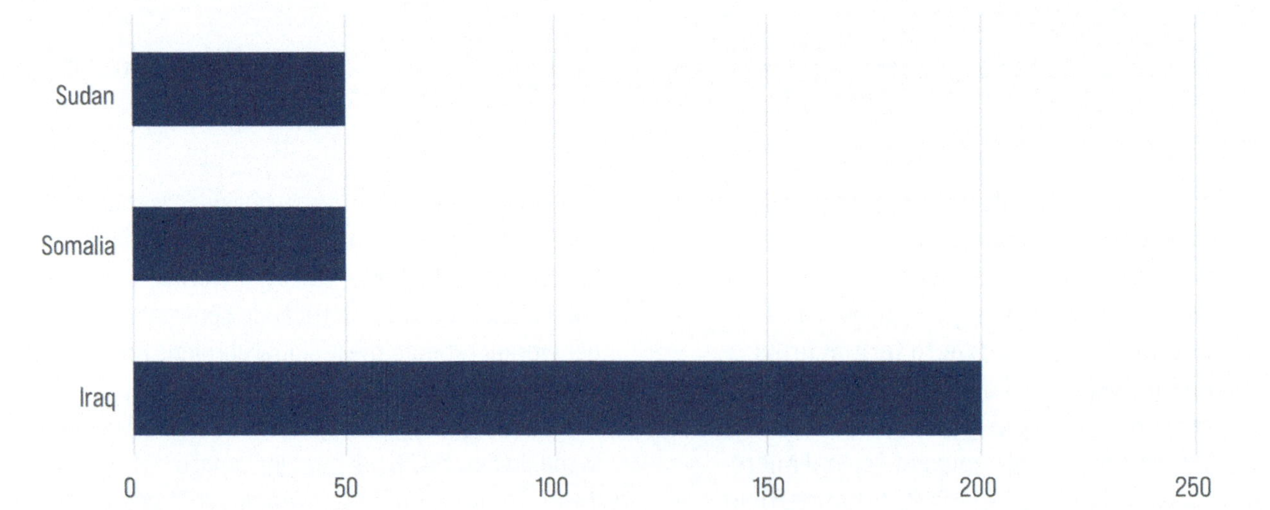

Source: ESCWA calculations based on informal sector enterprise surveys of Iraq, Somalia and the Sudan.

4. Challenges and barriers to transitioning to a formal economy in the Arab region

Evidence from Latin American countries indicates that robust and sustained economic growth can be instrumental in the gradual reduction of informal employment. Argentina, Brazil and Uruguay experienced significant economic expansion during the early 2000s, propelled by a combination of commodity booms, social policies, taxation and labour market reforms. This decade-long period was characterized by a steady decline in informal employment, coinciding with an increase in formal job creation, rising wages and enhanced social protection measures.

In Brazil, for example, between 2003 and 2013, the average annual gross domestic product (GDP) growth rate was approximately 4 per cent, driven by heightened global demand for commodities, notably soy and iron ore. The Government also instituted programmes such as Bolsa Família and labour market formalization policies, which incentivized businesses to register their workers. Consequently, the informality rate decreased from around 54 per cent to 45 per cent in the span of a decade.[21] Similarly, Uruguay, characterized by a robust institutional framework and an expansion of social security, experienced a substantial decline in informality, decreasing from 40.7 per cent in 2004 to 23.5 per cent in 2014. This improvement can be attributed to economic growth and the implementation of active labour market policies, including the application of the Monotax system which combined taxation with social security benefits that facilitated the integration of workers into formal employment.[22] While economic growth is a critical driver of formalization, it must be sustained over several years and accompanied by policies that actively promote labour inclusion.

In the Arab region,[23] economic growth has not translated into sufficient quality employment or a reduction in informality. While several countries have experienced growth booms, often driven by oil price hikes, large-scale infrastructure spending, or remittance and aid inflows, these cycles have been erratic and lacked structural transformation. Between 2000 and 2022, average real GDP growth in the region was 3.5 per cent, yet unemployment remained persistently high at around 10.7 per cent, with youth unemployment exceeding 25 per cent, the highest rate globally.[24] Unlike Latin America, where private sector development and industrial diversification have seen moderate progress, economies in the Arab region remain characterized by low private sector contribution to employment (less than 40 per cent) and underdeveloped manufacturing sectors (less than 12 per cent of GDP in most non-Gulf Cooperation Council States).[25] The region's growth has been neither inclusive nor sustained, largely due to the absence of comprehensive labour market reforms, weak small- and medium-sized enterprise (SME) ecosystems, and rigid employment regulations. Consequently, structural unemployment and informality, which affect over 60 per cent of workers in some countries, persist, undermining long-term job creation and social stability.[26]

The heterogeneity of informal employment across countries and demographic groups demands tailored, context-specific policies that consider the unique economic, institutional, cultural and gender-related characteristics of each country. The requirements and procedures for formalizing informal businesses, including own-account workers, differ from those necessary to formalize informal employment, regardless of whether such employment occurs within the formal or informal sectors.[27] For instance, incentives aimed at the self-employed or informal enterprises should prioritize aspects such as registration and licensing, tax compliance, adherence to regulations, and the benefits associated with formalization. The incentives and penalties for employers of informal workers, whether in informal or formal sectors, may necessitate a different approach. These should emphasize the extension of social protection benefits, the safeguarding of labour rights, and the enhancement of job quality. The tangible advantages of transitioning to a formal economy, such as access to finance, services, training initiatives, or social protection, are not readily apparent to informal workers or enterprises.[28]

According to a World Bank study,[29] firms operating in the informal sector cite a lack of access to finance as the most significant obstacle they encounter. One of the primary indicators of financial inclusion is the ownership of bank accounts, often viewed as a preliminary step for individuals to access a broader array of financial services, such as loans, investment and insurance. Bank accounts also function as essential tools for managing resources and mitigating financial risks to which actors in the informal sector are particularly vulnerable.

The finances of informal businesses typically operate outside formal financial channels. Owning a bank account legitimizes financial transactions and diminishes dependence on cash-based systems or reliance on internal funds or informal sources such as family and friends. Nonetheless, even when bank accounts are established, the absence of collateral or property ownership, insufficient documentation, and a lack of credit history present substantial obstacles that exacerbate financial exclusion for many informal economic units. Unstable income and an inability to secure financing can adversely affect business operations and impede growth.[30]

In Egypt, cash-based transactions are prevalent due to the lack of legal restrictions on the maximum allowable amount for such transactions. It is estimated that approximately 40 per cent of cash-based transactions occur within the informal sector.[31] In an effort to promote financial inclusion and facilitate the transition towards formalization, the Egyptian Government passed Law No. 18 of 2019 to regulate non-cash payment methods by placing specific caps on many types of cash transactions thus obliging individuals and establishments to use non-cash-based payments beyond stipulated amounts. The regulation also imposed certain penalties on non-compliance.[32] This law was paralleled with the Government's efforts to promote financial inclusion through digitization and mobile-based payments.[33] The Central Bank of Egypt also launched several programmes aimed at improving access to financing and providing loans at subsidized interest rates of 5 per cent.[34]

For small informal businesses, as well as for formal enterprises that employ a significant proportion of informal workers, the financial burdens associated with compliance with labour laws, coupled with increased operational costs related to enhanced salaries and benefits such as healthcare and social security, can sometimes outweigh the advantages of formalization.[35] Fear of increased taxation and additional financial burdens associated with formalization dissuades informal actors from transitioning.[36]

However, street vendors and waste collectors, for example, may find formalization feasible when the anticipated benefits, such as a consistent income, fundamental rights, access to credit, and legal and social protection, surpass the costs related to licensing, taxation and regulatory compliance.[37]

Box 1. Waste collectors in Brazil

In Brazil, the formalization of waste collectors, locally known as *catadores*, has been a significant development in integrating these workers into the country's waste management system. This process has involved official recognition, policy implementation, and the establishment of cooperatives to improve working conditions and social inclusion.[a]

In 2002, Brazil officially recognized waste picking as a legitimate occupation by including it in the Brazilian Classification of Occupations. This acknowledgment was a crucial step towards integrating waste collectors into formal labour frameworks. The approval of the National Solid Waste Policy in 2010 marked another milestone. The National Solid Waste Policy established shared responsibility for the product life cycle, outlining obligations for municipalities, the Federal District and generating companies in post-consumption reverse logistics. This policy framework provided a foundation for incorporating waste collectors into formal waste management processes.[b] The formation of waste collector cooperatives has been instrumental in the formalization process. These cooperatives not only organize collection and recycling activities but also advocate for better working conditions and fair compensation. Collaborations with private enterprises have further supported formalization efforts.

Despite advancements, challenges remain. The costs associated with formalization, such as licensing fees and compliance with regulations, can be prohibitive for some waste collectors. For some, the benefits of formalization, such as access to credit or legal protection, may not always outweigh these costs, particularly for those operating independently. It is essential to design formalization processes that are inclusive and considerate of the economic realities faced by waste collectors.[c]

[a] International Alliance of Waste Pickers, Waste Pickers in Brazil, n.d.

[b] Springer Nature, Green Jobs and Social Rights: A Case Study on the Formalization of Waste Pickers in Latin America, 2024, p. 133–152.

[c] Manuel Rosaldo, Top-Down and Bottom-Up Formalization: Waste Pickers' Struggles for Labour Rights in São Paulo and Bogotá, 2023, ILR Review, 77(1), 32-61.

Data derived from informal enterprise surveys conducted in Somalia and the Sudan indicate that formalization facilitates access to markets and credit opportunities. A significant proportion of business owners operating informal enterprises in Somalia (62.1 per cent) and the Sudan (57.9 per cent) recognized access to potential customers as a primary advantage of registering their businesses. Nearly half of the respondents in the Sudan (49.3 per cent) and Somalia (46.3 per cent) cited enhanced access to loans as a substantial benefit of formal registration. In Iraq, formal registration is regarded as a protective measure against corruption, with the reduction of bribes identified as the most significant benefit (55.8 per cent). As these findings show, formalization can play a role in fostering trust in institutions and establishing a more transparent operational environment.[38]

Figure 10. Perceived benefits of business registration across countries

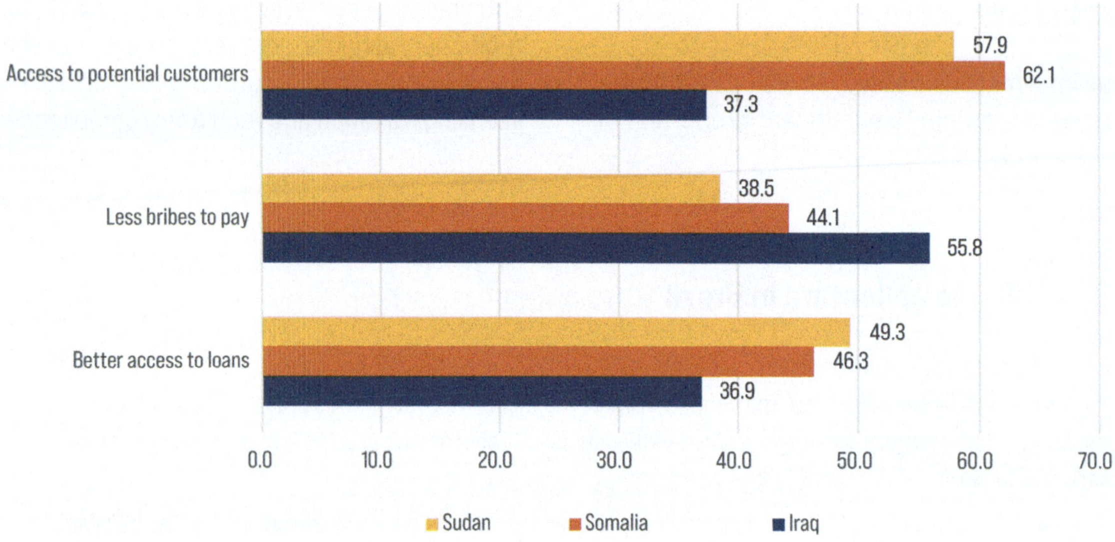

Source: ESCWA calculations based on informal sector enterprise surveys of Iraq, Somalia and the Sudan.

Some informal enterprises choose to remain within the informal sector due to the increased flexibility and minimal regulatory oversight. For instance, for a street vendor, formalization may not substantially enhance income or working conditions, particularly if their clientele primarily consists of low-income individuals. The costly and time-consuming nature of business registration, cumbersome licensing processes, bureaucratic red tape, the financial burden of taxation, along with the necessity to adhere to complex regulations and post-formalization standards, deter businesses from transitioning to the formal economy.[39] A number of Governments in the region have embarked on regulatory and legal reforms to alleviate the burden.

The Jordanian Government initiated the Investor Journey Reform programme in 2021, aimed at enhancing government to business service delivery, increasing efficiency in both business and government operations, reducing compliance costs and time, and improving the predictability of the business environment. To foster better coordination among government agencies involved throughout the business lifecycle, as well as to simplify, unify and expedite business registration and licensing procedures, the International Standard Industrial Classification of All Economic Activities (ISIC) 4 classification framework was implemented for newly registered businesses.[40] In 2022, the Integrated Business Registry System was introduced to streamline the registration process through a single window at the Companies Control Department.[41]

In 2017, the Egyptian Government enacted Law No. 15/2017, which pertains to the simplification of the procedures for licensing industrial installations. This legislation substantially reduced the bureaucratic requirements and time necessary for the establishment of industrial facilities, decreasing the duration from 600 days to 7 days for industries deemed to pose low risks to health, the environment, safety or security, and to 30 days for facilities classified as high risk.[42] The Egyptian Government also enacted Law 152/2020, which established a framework to encourage micro-, small- and medium-sized enterprise (MSME) formalization by granting enterprises that seek to regularize their status a 5-year exemption from stamp duty and registration fees, as well as a comprehensive tax amnesty for all outstanding taxes, in addition to various non-tax incentives. The duration required to obtain an operating license in Egypt was also reduced to fewer than 14 days. These initiatives were further reinforced by the establishment of the MSME Development Agency, designed as a one-stop shop to expedite and facilitate the procedures necessary for obtaining startup approval.

The adoption of the Financial Inclusion Strategy (2022-2025) of Egypt aimed to improve access to financial and non-financial services for MSMEs and startups. Similarly, new legislation (149/2023) empowers the Industrial Development Authority to issue temporary 3-year working permits to unregistered industrial enterprises, contingent upon their compliance with environmental regulations, civil procedures and related inspections. Throughout the 3-year period, the company is afforded the opportunity to formalize its structure and personnel.[43]

At the regional level, as of 2019, the average cost of initiating a business was 15.91 per cent per capita gross national income, indicating a substantial financial obstacle for numerous entrepreneurs. Lebanon exhibited the highest cost at 42.3 per cent of per capita gross national income, underscoring the disproportionate challenges encountered in high-cost environments. Bahrain presented a cost of merely 1 per cent. In addition to financial considerations, the average duration required to establish a business in the region was 19.6 days, with Lebanon requiring 15 days and Bahrain only 8.5 days, reflecting the significant disparities in the efficiency of regulatory frameworks.[44]

Inadequate legal frameworks impede the formalization of businesses and labour by establishing barriers that are challenging to surmount. Weak governance, distrust in public institutions, and perceptions of corruption further exacerbate tax evasion and the reliance on bribery to circumvent formal channels.[45] The manner in which regulations are enforced frequently constitutes a significant source of administrative barriers. Centralization, coupled with weak, inconsistent or selective enforcement capacities, neglect and perceived unfair treatment by formal institutions, contributes to a deterioration of trust. Confusing, overlapping or outdated laws often lead to ambiguity regarding the requirements for businesses to transition into the formal economy.[46,47]

Tax rates in the Arab region vary significantly across countries. Most tax regimes, however, are not sufficiently streamlined to accommodate small businesses, which often operate on narrow profit margins. High tax rates or complex tax filing processes may deter small, informal businesses from formal registration, particularly if the perceived benefits of formalization do not outweigh these challenges.[48] For instance, uniform tax rates applied across businesses of varying sizes do not take into consideration the financial constraints faced by smaller enterprises, rendering compliance both financially and administratively burdensome.

Despite a series of legal reforms, the business environment in Egypt remains restrictive and the considerable burden of licensing obligations on firms, along with the regulatory and tax burdens associated with formalization, remains a significant impediment to economic activity. The substantial costs associated with compliance have a particularly pronounced effect on micro and small enterprises, which constitute the majority of the Egyptian commercial landscape and operate with limited resources. Despite attempts to calibrate regulations according to the size of the company, such measures are often ineffective, as they may inadvertently discourage the growth of smaller firms or lead to unintended consequences, such as the underreporting of sales or personnel once a certain threshold is reached.[49]

The World Bank Enterprise Survey indicated that in 2013, 31.2 per cent of enterprises in Jordan identified "access to finance" as the primary impediment to the business environment. However, by 2019, this figure had declined significantly to 2.2 per cent. A considerable proportion of enterprises continued to perceive tax rates as a significant barrier in both years. Jordan lacks a distinct tax structure for small businesses. Depending on their business classification, MSMEs are subject to the same taxation as individuals with personal income or larger enterprises. Personal income taxes are levied on self-employed individuals, as well as MSMEs, rather than corporate income taxes. Individuals benefit from a 9,000 Jordanian dinar (JD) income exemption, while families with dependents qualify for an exemption of up to JD 23,000. MSMEs that are registered as self-employed are exempt from income taxes if their annual business revenue does not exceed JD 23,000.[50]

In Iraq, an informal sector enterprise survey indicated that nearly two-thirds of the owners of informal businesses interviewed hoped to avoid the informal payments or bribes associated with formalization. Over two-thirds indicated a preference to evade tax obligations. Avoidance of government inspections is another common rationale for not formalizing, particularly among home-based enterprises. Nearly 45 per cent of firms cited the time-consuming and costly nature of registration as a significant disincentive.[51]

In the Sudan, the informal sector enterprise survey identified the primary reason for the failure to register informal businesses as concern regarding tax obligations. This was followed by the absence of perceived benefits, lack of information, and the time-consuming nature of registration processes, associated fees and paperwork.[52]

Social, cultural and political barriers also significantly impede the transition process. Deeply entrenched cultural practices and social norms may be behind resistance to formalization,[53] as informal arrangements are often perceived as more culturally accommodating and community-focused. Informal structures typically rely on personal relationships, community support and flexibility, which are viewed as more amenable than formal structures. Informal structures predominantly depend on community networks for trade, employment and credit, aligning closely with communal values and traditions. This alignment can render formalization as intrusive or unnecessary. Informal actors express concerns that formalization may result in a loss of immediate cash flow or an increased risk of job loss, or may compromise flexibility by imposing rigid processes that small and micro enterprises often find overwhelming.

5. Forecasting informal employment and evaluating policy interventions: The case of Egypt

With persistently high levels of informal employment, Egypt represents a pertinent case for the study of informality and the evaluation of policy interventions, while also providing insights that may be applicable to other countries in the region confronted by similar challenges. To forecast the impact of relevant exogenous variables on the informal employment rate in Egypt, an ARIMAX[54] model was developed. Egypt was selected as a case study due to the availability of reliable and comprehensive datasets on informal employment sourced from the ILO database and labour force surveys. Collectively, these datasets offer a sufficient number of observations to ensure the consistency and validity of the analysis. The selection of exogenous variables was based on their theoretical relevance and the availability of time-series data.

The ARIMAX model extends the autoregressive integrated moving average framework by incorporating external predictors (exogenous variables) alongside time-series components. It captures relationships within the data through autoregressive and moving average terms, while simultaneously accounting for the influence of external factors. The model is represented by the following equation:

$$Y_t=\phi_1 Y_{t-1}+\theta_1 \varepsilon_{t-1}+\beta_1\cdot \text{StartupCost}_t+\beta_2\cdot \text{TaxRate}_t+\beta_3\cdot \text{GDPGrowth}_t+\beta_4\cdot \text{Inflation}_t$$
$$+\beta_5\cdot \text{ExchangeVoatility}_t+\beta_6\cdot \text{PopGrowth}_t+\varepsilon_t$$

Where:

- Yt: informal employment rate at time t.
- ϕ_1: Coefficient of the autoregressive term (past value Y{t-1}).
- θ_1: Coefficient of the moving average term (past error ε_{t-1}).
- β_1 to β_6: Coefficients for exogenous variables.
- StartupCostt: Cost of business start-up procedures at time t.
- TaxRatet: Corporate tax rate at time t.
- GDPGrowtht: GDP growth rate at time t.
- Inflationt: Inflation rate at time t.
- ExchangeVolatilityt: Exchange rate volatility at time t.
- PopGrowtht: Population growth rate at time t.
- εt: Error term (white noise).

The exogenous variables selected for the model comprise: the cost of business start-up procedures, corporate tax rate, GDP growth, inflation rate, exchange rate volatility and population growth, all of which were chosen due to their relevance in influencing the dynamics of informal employment.

Elevated costs, tax burdens and macroeconomic volatility frequently drive the prevalence of informality, while growth-related factors are critical for promoting the creation of formal employment opportunities. Although other indicators, such as social protection coverage, education levels and access to credit, are acknowledged to impact informal employment, they were excluded from the model owing to the unavailability of data throughout the study period.

A. Model specification

Data preprocessing was conducted to ensure completeness and consistency through various techniques, including the management of missing values, stabilization of the series, and application of transformations where necessary. Assessing stationarity constituted a fundamental step, which was evaluated using visual inspection of the time series and the Augmented Dickey-Fuller test. For non-stationary series, differencing (d=1) was employed to achieve stationarity. The model orders (p,d,q) were established through the autocorrelation function and partial autocorrelation function plots. A pronounced drop-off in the autocorrelation function after lag 1 indicated a moving average term of order q=1, while a significant spike at lag 1 in the partial autocorrelation function suggested an autoregressive term of order p=1. Based on this analysis, an ARIMAX (1,1,1) model was selected. To ensure model adequacy, a comprehensive residual analysis was conducted. The Ljung-Box test for residual autocorrelation yielded p-values greater than 0.05 for all tested lags (1–10), indicating that the residuals behave akin to white noise. Normality tests, including the Shapiro-Wilk Test (p=0.974) and the Jarque-Bera Test (p=0.879), confirmed that the residuals conformed to a normal distribution. The model's performance was assessed using accuracy metrics, which included a root mean square error of 0.451 and a mean absolute error of 0.342. These low error values corroborate that the model fits the data effectively.

B. Results and findings

In the baseline scenario, the ARIMAX model was used to forecast the informal employment rate for the period 2024–2030, under the assumption that all exogenous variables would remain constant at their last observed values throughout the forecast period. The projected trend illustrates the expected evolution of the informal employment rate over time, providing a foundational reference for comparison against potential policy interventions or changes in economic conditions. This is visually represented in the graph below.

Figure 11. Informal employment rate 2008-2030 (Percentage)

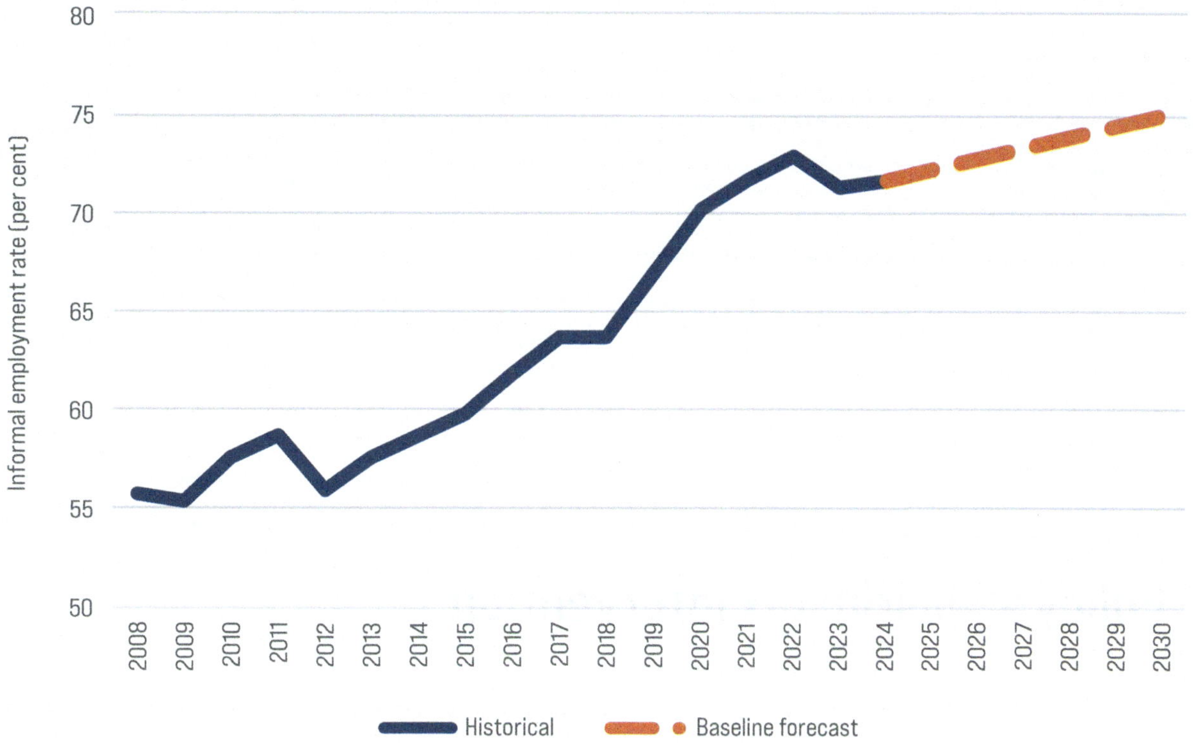

Source: Data for 2008–2019 and 2023 were compiled from ILOSTAT, data for 2020–2022 were calculated by ESCWA based on labour force surveys, and data for 2024–2030 are ESCWA calculations based on the ARIMAX model.

Historically, the rate of informal employment has exhibited a gradual upward trend, characterized by minor fluctuations, commencing at 55.73 per cent in 2008 and escalating to 71.33 per cent by 2023. Projections for the period 2024–2030 indicate a continued increase in informal employment, beginning at 71.9 per cent in 2024 and culminating at 75.16 per cent by 2030.

This consistent rise is reflective of structural challenges associated with reducing informality in the absence of significant policy interventions. The historical and forecasted trends highlight the urgent need for targeted measures addressing the drivers contributing to informality and fostering formal job creation to mitigate this escalating trend.

Table 2. Coefficients and significance of exogenous variables

Variable	Coefficient	p-value	Significant
Cost of start-up procedures	0.115	0.062	No
Corporate tax rate	-0.028	0.042	Yes
GDP growth	-0.091	0.018	Yes
Inflation rate	0.003	0.774	No
Exchange rate volatility	0.012	0.015	Yes
Population growth	-0.023	0.083	No
Unemployment rate	-0.151	0.01	Yes

Source: ESCWA calculations using the ARIMAX model. Exogenous variables were obtained from the World Bank (cost of start-up procedures, GDP growth, inflation rate), ILOSTAT (unemployment rate), UN DESA (population growth), IMF International Financial Statistics (exchange rate volatility), and Egyptian Tax Authority (corporate tax rate).

The results indicate that the corporate tax rate, GDP growth and exchange rate volatility are statistically significant at the 5 per cent level. The corporate tax rate exhibits a significant negative effect on the informal employment rate, suggesting that a reduction in the tax rate could substantially decrease informal employment. GDP growth and exchange rate volatility are critical factors in influencing informal employment, consistent with economic theory. While the cost of business start-up procedures aligns with theoretical expectations in suggesting that higher costs incentivize informality, the coefficient is not statistically significant at 5 per cent. Similarly, population growth and the inflation rate do not serve as significant predictors within this model.

C. Policy scenario: tax intervention

Figure 12. Forecasts of informal employment rate, 2024-2030 - baseline scenario compared to policy scenario (Percentage)

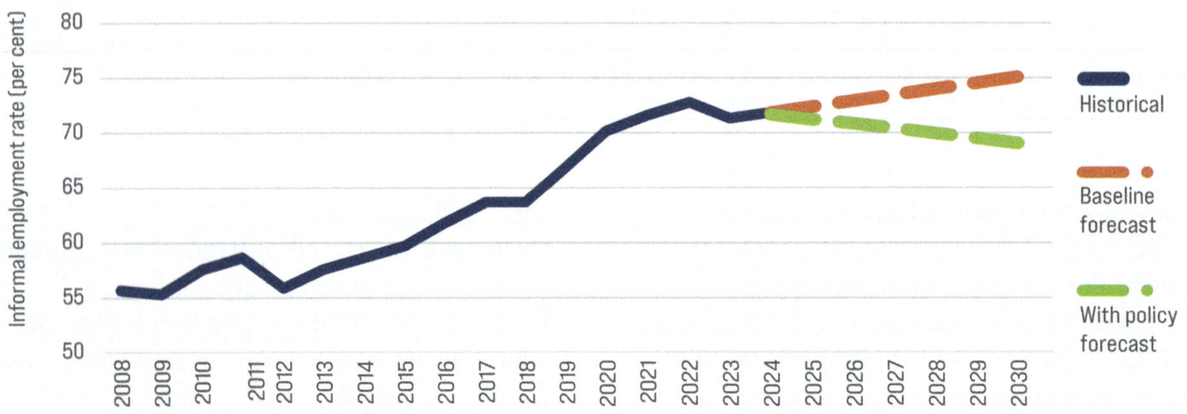

Source: Data for 2008–2019 and 2023 were compiled from ILOSTAT, data for 2020–2022 were calculated by ESCWA based on labour force surveys, and data for 2024–2030 are ESCWA calculations based on the ARIMAX model.

Given its significance in the model, the corporate tax rate was selected as a key policy indicator to evaluate its impact on the informal employment rate. By constructing a policy scenario in which the corporate tax rate decreases by 2 percentage points annually, while all other exogenous variables remain constant at their last observed values, the potential effects of this tax intervention were assessed. The ARIMAX model was rerun under this scenario, and the results illustrate the projected changes in the informal employment rate over the period 2024–2030.

The policy scenario renders a consistent decline in the informal employment rate in comparison to the baseline forecast. By the year 2030, the informal employment rate is anticipated to be 6.07 percentage points lower (69.09 per cent) than under the baseline scenario (75.16 per cent). The cumulative impact of the tax reduction becomes increasingly salient over time, with the disparity expanding from 0.20 percentage points in 2024 to 5.86 percentage points by 2030. A gradual reduction in corporate tax rates is shown to be a viable policy instrument to promote business formalization and mitigate informal employment. Although the short-term effects may be modest, the long-term implications are substantial, demonstrating the need for consistent and sustained policy implementation.

Data-driven forecasting models, such as ARIMAX, can play a critical role in the analysis of the persistent challenges of informal employment. By incorporating key exogenous variables, ranging from macroeconomic indicators to fiscal policies, the model not only provides robust projections of informal employment trends but also offers evidence-based insights into the potential effectiveness of targeted policy interventions.

The baseline forecast reveals a concerning trajectory, with informal employment expected to rise steadily through 2030. However, the policy scenario incorporating corporate tax reductions demonstrates that well-calibrated interventions can yield meaningful results. A sustained decrease in corporate tax rates not only slows the growth of informal employment but also significantly lowers the informality rate over time.

These findings carry important implications for policymakers in Egypt and across the Arab region. They show that tackling informality requires more than isolated measures; it demands a strategic, long-term approach that leverages fiscal reforms, fosters economic growth, and reduces barriers to formalization. This case study reaffirms the transformative potential of evidence-based policy design, paving the way for just and effective transitions from informal to formal economies.

6. Global and regional examples of just transitions

While it is challenging to identify a linear and irreversible transition process, experiences from various countries around the globe provide empirical evidence and lessons learned from successful attempts at reducing informality and initiating a process of just transition to formal structures. These interventions encompass a range of measures, including the use of technology, tax reforms, governance improvement, labour market regulations and mechanisms to facilitate financing.

A. In the Arab region

1. Morocco

The auto-entrepreneur programme in Morocco, launched in 2015, promotes youth entrepreneurship and helps regulate the informal sector by simplifying administrative procedures and offering financial incentives. It enables freelancers to register, legalize their work, access health insurance, and pay minimal taxes. In the first six years, nearly half a million individual business registrations were submitted.[55]

The programme's user-friendly registration system, accessible through local post-office agencies, simplified formalization, especially for micro entrepreneurs in rural areas. The low, fixed tax rate (1 per cent for industrial, commercial and craft activities; 2 per cent for service providers) made formalization financially attractive. Auto-entrepreneurs gained access to health insurance, pensions and social security, and were thus provided with essential protection previously unavailable to informal workers.[56] Effective outreach, the use of digital tools, regional accessibility and strong institutional partnerships were key success factors.

National campaigns to promote the programme highlighted the benefits of formalization, such as government support, market credibility and reduced risks, addressing concerns about awareness and eligibility. The programme's nationwide accessibility increased participation in marginalized regions, while digital tools streamlined account management and tax payments. Early successes created a snowball effect, encouraging more entrepreneurs to transition from the informal sector.

Morocco also hosts a number of successful local examples in rural areas where targeted formalization initiatives have had success, especially in rural women's entrepreneurship and empowerment. Box 2 illustrates one of these examples which could be beneficially upscaled at the national level.

Box 2. Transitioning from informality to formality: the Tizwa project

The Tizwa project showcases initiatives that combine innovation, training and collaboration to empower rural women to overcome barriers and integrate into the formal economy.

Rural Moroccan women who work in beekeeping, hospitality, handicrafts and other vocations face significant challenges, with 68 per cent engaged in the informal economy. This sector, marked by low income, instability and a lack of social protection, limits opportunities for growth. Cultural norms, limited education and resource scarcity aggravate these barriers, hampering women's economic autonomy.

The Tizwa project provides training and education on life skills, entrepreneurship and technical knowledge in business management, finance and marketing; mentorship by experienced professionals who guide participants through project implementation and sustainability; infrastructure development by supporting solar energy, water access and one-stop hubs for business creation; and policy support by offering financial incentives, simplified administrative processes and cooperative promotion to streamline the transition.

The project follows a three-pronged approach that includes an ideation phase to identify viable business ideas through coaching and collaboration; an incubation phase to refine business plans, acquire skills and secure resources; and a mentoring phase to personalize guidance and networking to integrate participants into formal markets.

The initiative saw 95.83 per cent of participants successfully transition to formal businesses by launching entrepreneurship projects, boosting local economies. Businesses varied between agricultural ventures, handicrafts and artisanship, food and hospitality services, and tourism and cultural enterprises. Women reported increased economic independence and reduced cultural barriers.

Source: Meriem Rhoflane and Chaimae Bourjij, The Transition from the Informal to the Formal Economy: Case Study of the Tizwa Project in the Village of Aït Ben Haddou, 2023, Friedrich Naumann Foundation for Freedom.

3. Tunisia

Tunisia has the lowest informal employment rate in the region and is recognized for its advanced social protection efforts. A key innovation in reducing informality was the implementation of social solidarity structures through the social and solidarity economy law, which promotes formalization. Informal employment is concentrated in labour-intensive, low-productivity sectors like agriculture, construction, handicrafts, retail and domestic work. The social and solidarity economy law, enacted between 2020 and 2021, led to the creation of the Tunisian Social and Solidarity Economy Authority, which facilitates the integration of informal units, particularly in agriculture and handicrafts. Further investment and policy support remain key for long-term success.[57]

Tunisia supports informal businesses by improving access to social protection, organizing workers into cooperatives, and leveraging digital tools for registration and payments. The agricultural service cooperatives (Sociétés Mutuelles de Services Agricoles) play a key role in integrating informal farmers into formal markets by providing access to credit, resources, training and social protection. Established as social enterprises, they have helped producers enhance productivity and formalize operations despite challenges in scale, financial autonomy and membership growth.[58] While the Sociétés Mutuelles de Services Agricoles represent a promising and innovative approach to local development, they remain constrained in terms of scope, financial autonomy and a hesitant membership base. Nevertheless, their early achievements indicate that there is a demand for reliable structures and orderly transitions within certain informal sectors.

The social and solidarity economy law has legitimized informal entities, granting them access to funding and support mechanisms. As informal employment remains widespread, sustained efforts are needed to overcome systemic barriers and scale successful initiatives. Cooperatives, when combined with supportive policies, have proven effective in facilitating transitions to the formal sector. Tunisia leads the region in integrating informal workers, reducing informal employment in key sectors to below 50 per cent.

Other global experiences present distinct narratives but with similar intentions and objectives.

B. In Africa

1. Nigeria

To encourage informal units to formalize, a comprehensive strategy was developed that encompasses the expansion of social protection programmes, education and skill development, economic diversification for the self-employed, and the enforcement of labour standards.[59] The primary emphasis was on formalization efforts for MSMEs. These efforts comprised measures such as the establishment of a national business council, the Presidential Enabling Business Environment Council, to streamline registration processes through initiatives like a 60-day national action plan designed to alleviate bottlenecks. Subsequently, the Council implemented executive orders to enhance transparency and efficiency within the business environment and to address procedural challenges. The comprehensive approach included financial incentives, such as tax holidays for startups and certain sectors, including agriculture and e-commerce, as well as access to government-backed credit facilities contingent upon formal registration. It also incorporated awareness-raising campaigns aimed at educating entrepreneurs on the advantages of formalization, although the effectiveness of these campaigns has shown variability. A notable aspect of this strategy is the support for women entrepreneurs, facilitated by efforts to replicate Law 2125 of Colombia (box 3), which incentivizes formalization for women-led businesses.

Despite a concerted effort to promote formalization, numerous obstacles continue to impede progress, including the coexistence of various formal and informal levies and taxes which increases operational costs without corresponding enhancements in infrastructure or services. Also, frequent changes in government administrations have led to inconsistent policy application, thereby creating uncertainty for businesses.[60]

Box 3. Law 2125 in Colombia

On 4 August 2021, Columbia passed Law 2125 to promote the creation, formalization and strengthening of MSMEs led by women. It establishes incentives and a public policy framework to enhance women's entrepreneurial capacities, close gender gaps, and improve their participation in the national economy.

The law mandates that women-led enterprises in the informal sector must formalize their business registration to access benefits such as financial support. Chambers of commerce are tasked with facilitating formalization through dedicated sessions. The law provides for women informal vendors with at least five years of experience to be eligible for benefits, provided they formalize their businesses. The law stipulates that government agencies must simplify regulatory processes, such as tax registration, to encourage women entrepreneurs to formalize their enterprises.

The law prioritizes groups such as victims of armed conflict, rural women, indigenous communities and informal vendors, offering them tailored incentives for transitioning to formal employment or entrepreneurship. Financial institutions are required to develop methodologies to assess credit risks for women-led MSMEs, mitigating barriers to obtaining loans. Microcredits guaranteed up to 90 per cent of their value are provided through the National Guarantee Fund. As part of the formalization process, newly transitioned businesses receive a distinctive certification mark for formalized women-led enterprises, creating visibility and market incentives. Partnerships between public and private sectors are encouraged so as to enhance financial inclusion and entrepreneurial support.

The law promotes training and mentorship programmes through the National Training Service and other entities, targeting women entrepreneurs and students. It also introduces an annual National Women's Entrepreneurship Week to celebrate and promote women-led businesses, as well as an awards initiative in an effort to reduce gender gaps in entrepreneurship. The law stipulates explicit support for women affected by armed conflict and calls for reintegration programmes by fostering entrepreneurial opportunities tied to societal reconciliation efforts.

Source: Función Pública, Law 2125 of 2021, available at https://www-funcionpublica-gov-co.translate.goog/eva/gestornormativo/norma.php?i=168050&_x_tr_sl=es&_x_tr_tl=en&_x_tr_hl=en&_x_tr_pto=sc (accessed on 20 January 2025).

2. Ghana

Ghana has implemented institutional support, tax incentives[61] and business development services to promote formalization. A range of tax incentives has been offered to businesses to facilitate their transition into the formal economy, particularly in sectors such as agriculture, manufacturing (notably businesses engaged in export trade or utilizing local raw materials), construction, mining and tourism. These incentives aim to alleviate the tax burden on businesses, thereby rendering formalization more attractive and economically viable. Authorities have introduced various services, including training programmes designed to enhance entrepreneurs' skills in business management and operations, access to finance to establish connections between MSMEs and financial institutions to improve credit accessibility, market access initiatives to aid businesses in identifying and entering new domestic and international markets, and advisory services to enhance business processes and ensure compliance with regulatory standards.

C. In Latin America

Latin American countries present rich and diverse experiences in transitioning from informal employment, albeit with mixed outcomes.

1. Argentina

Over 40 per cent of the workforce in Argentina operates informally,[62] primarily in agriculture, construction and domestic service. Informality is concentrated in small and micro enterprises with fewer than 10 employees. To address this, the Government implemented policies to integrate informal workers into formal employment through productive development programmes, fiscal incentives, labour inspections and streamlined business registration processes. Efforts also focused on reducing regional and urban-rural disparities by expanding social security, health insurance and pensions for informal workers. Early results showed increased social security coverage, particularly in urban areas, and some reduction in regional inequalities. However, challenges persist, especially in rural areas, agriculture and domestic work, requiring more targeted and sustained interventions.

2. Mexico

Approximately 55 per cent of the total workforce in Mexico is informal,[63] with informality rates among indigenous populations exceeding 70 per cent. Government efforts have focused on reducing informality in regions with high indigenous populations by implementing strategies to improve income distribution and enhance access to social protection for marginalized groups. This two-pronged approach included initiatives aimed at improving job quality alongside programmes that provided training and upskilling opportunities to facilitate the transition of informal workers to formal employment.

Early findings indicated an increase in social protection coverage among informal workers in specific regions, along with improved income distribution and access to essential services for marginalized populations. However, due to the limited enforcement of labour standards in remote areas, high rates of informality persisted in rural regions and among indigenous communities. The conclusion drawn from this experience is that education and skill-building programmes are essential for equipping informal workers to transition into the formal labour market.

3. Peru

Over 70 per cent of the employed population in Peru works informally,[64] with the highest rates observed in rural areas and among women, where informal employment predominates in agriculture, mining and urban microenterprises. Considered a leader in prioritizing informality in development discussions, recent efforts have concentrated on rural informality, focusing on extending labour rights to agricultural workers and small-scale producers through targeted initiatives. These initiatives emphasize labour rights and social protection. This has been coupled with the implementation of policies designed to formalize micro and small enterprises. The Government introduced financial and technical assistance programmes aimed at helping informal micro and small enterprises register and comply with labour regulations. Additional initiatives seek to integrate informal workers into formal employment by linking them to value chains and larger markets.

Significant progress in the formalization of rural workers has been made, with a noticeable increase in the participation of small enterprises in formal economic activities. Despite this encouraging progress, high levels of informality remain prevalent in small-scale agriculture and artisanal activities, and formalization policies had limited effectiveness in remote regions.

D. In Asia

1. India

The informal sector in India constitutes a significant part of the economy, with over 83.5 per cent of the workforce engaged in informal employment as of 2017–2018. This primarily includes agriculture, construction and domestic work, with agriculture being the dominant employer in rural areas. Informal employment is categorized into lower-tier (e.g., agricultural labourers, street vendors) and upper-tier (e.g., electricians, small entrepreneurs) jobs. Self-employment is widespread, particularly in small, unregistered enterprises.[65] Women, lower-caste groups, and workers with limited education are overrepresented in the informal sector.

Government initiatives have aimed to address these challenges. The Pradhan Mantri Shram Yogi Maan-Dhan scheme provides voluntary pensions for informal workers earning less than 15,000 Indian rupees per month, and the Ayushman Bharat scheme offers health insurance coverage of up to 500,000 Indian rupees per family annually. The Unorganized Workers' Social Security Act (2008) and the consolidation of labour laws into four simplified codes were measures aiming to enhance social protection and compliance.[66]

Financial inclusion efforts, such as the Jan Dhan Yojana initiative, have facilitated bank access and direct benefit transfers for informal workers. Digitization initiatives, including online business registration and the goods and services tax, have streamlined taxation and encouraged formalization. Skill development programmes under the Skill India Mission aim to enhance informal workers' employability in formal sectors. Mudra loans, for example, provide collateral-free credit to micro and small enterprises, while the Street Vendors Act (2014) safeguards their rights.[67]

Sector-specific measures have supported agriculture through farmer producer organizations and subsidies. Domestic work has been addressed through State-level initiatives promoting minimum wages and social protections. The e-Shram portal was developed as a national database to facilitate access to social security and training programmes.

These initiatives have led to notable progress, including 480 million Jan Dhan accounts, millions of workers enrolled in the Pradhan Mantri Shram Yogi Maan-Dhan and the Ayushman Bharat scheme, over 10 million persons trained under the Skill India Mission, and a substantial number of enterprises integrated into the tax system through goods and services tax registration. However, challenges persist, including high informality levels, ineffective enforcement of labour laws, bureaucratic inefficiencies, and exclusion from social protection programmes. Women in the informal sector face additional barriers, such as occupational segregation and inadequate childcare support. Strengthening enforcement mechanisms, raising awareness, and addressing gender-specific challenges remain crucial for advancing formalization efforts in India.

Table 3. Summary of selected regional and global interventions that encourage just transitions

Country	Tax regime	Social protection measure	Labour code reform	Simplified registration	Institutional reform	Value chain integration	Sector-specific intervention	Group targeting	Social and solidarity economy	Digital tools	Access to finance/credit
Morocco	*	*		*			*	*	*	*	*
Tunisia		*			*	*	*	*		*	
Egypt		*		*							*
Ghana	*				*	*					*
Nigeria	*	*	*	*	*		*			*	*
Argentina	*	*	*	*			*			*	*
Mexico	*	*					*	*		*	
Peru	*	*				*	*			*	
India	*	*	*	*	*	*	*	*		*	*

Source: Authors compilation.

E. Leveraging technology for just transitions

Several countries are using e-formalization to address certain challenges. Experiences from around the globe present diverse and innovative approaches to pioneering technology. Below are a few examples.

1. Cambodia

In December 2024, the Cambodian Government introduced a digital platform designed to support informal economy workers by enabling voluntary registration which allowed them to be formally recognized without the imposition of tax obligations. Registered workers obtain access to benefits including enrolment in the National Social Security Fund, healthcare services, skill development programmes, and formal financial services such as loans and investment capital. The initiative aims to enhance government support for informal workers by collecting accurate data to inform policy decisions and interventions.[68] The National Social Security Fund developed mobile applications to facilitate member access to social security services, to monitor work history, access transaction statements, locate nearby health facilities, and stay updated on Fund news. The Fund also collaborated with financial institutions to enable beneficiaries to pay their employees' monthly contributions to the Fund.[69] These digital initiatives and partnerships are intended to enhance the accessibility, efficiency and transparency of social security in Cambodia, benefiting both formal and informal workers.

2. Nigeria

Nigeria has developed TradeDepot,[70] a business-to-business e-commerce platform that connects small-scale informal retailers in Africa with major consumer goods manufacturers, thereby integrating them into formal supply chains and reducing operational costs. Informal retailers can order and pay for goods utilizing TradeDepot's mobile applications, receiving deliveries directly to their stores, which ensures consistent access to a wide range of products at competitive prices. These initiatives not only lower operational costs but also enhance the profitability and growth potential of informal retailers. Since its inception, TradeDepot has established a network of over 40,000 micro retailers who have reported significant improvements in revenue and business outcomes due to enhanced access to products and financial services.

3. Brazil

Simples Nacional is a simplified tax regime in Brazil designed to reduce bureaucracy and tax burdens for micro and small enterprises by consolidating various federal, State and municipal taxes into a single payment.[71] This initiative streamlines the tax process for eligible micro and small enterprises with a predetermined profit ceiling. The programme alleviates administrative burdens, offers reduced rates based on the company's revenue, potentially leading to significant tax savings, and simplifies accounting and compliance requirements. The platform is integrated with eSocial, a digital system that unifies and simplifies the reporting of labour, social security and tax information by employers. Businesses operating under Simples Nacional can efficiently report payroll, social security contributions and other mandatory data using eSocial. Together, both platforms establish a more business-friendly environment, particularly for small enterprises, by reducing complexity and promoting compliance.

4. Peru

The Electronic Payroll System in Peru is a digital platform designed to streamline the registration and management of employment data for both employers and employees.[72] The system was developed to encourage the transition of enterprises from informal to formal employment sectors. The system enhances the effectiveness of labour inspections, thereby ensuring compliance with labour regulations. Within a few years, the system successfully formalized around 70,000 workers.

5. Hungary

The Hungarian Simplified Employment Act streamlines the process of hiring for seasonal and casual work, particularly in sectors such as agriculture and tourism.[73] The legislation reduces administrative burdens by simplifying notifications, reporting and payment procedures associated with temporary employment. Employers can register simplified employment electronically or via text message, thereby facilitating legal compliance and mitigating informal labour practices. The Act aims to improve regulatory frameworks and enhance public service delivery through policy reform and digital innovation.

F. Emerging role of social solidarity structures in assuring just transitions

Cooperatives can facilitate formalization by providing legal and regulatory support, financial access, collective bargaining, market access, training, social protection and improved working conditions.

Examples from the Arab region illustrate how cooperatives have effectively paved the way for transition to formal employment by enhancing the livelihoods and economic security of their members. In Egypt, agricultural cooperatives provide farmers with access to credit, agricultural inputs (such as seeds and fertilizers) and training in modern farming techniques. These cooperatives also assist farmers in marketing their products collectively, ensuring better prices and reducing reliance on intermediaries. By participating in these cooperatives, farmers can formalize their agricultural activities, gain access to formal credit, and benefit from economies of scale.[74]

Box 4. Other solidarity-based interventions

Grameen Bank (Bangladesh): While not a cooperative itself, Grameen Bank's microfinance model has inspired many savings and credit cooperatives that provide financial services to informal workers, helping them formalize their economic activities.

Self-Employed Women's Association (India): The Association is a trade union of women workers in the informal sector that operates as a cooperative. It helps members obtain fair wages, social security and access to healthcare, formalizing their employment.

Cooperative of Coffee Farmers (Colombia): Coffee cooperatives in Colombia help small-scale farmers access international markets, secure better prices, and adhere to fair trade standards, which leads to the formalization of their operations.

Kenya Dairy Farmers Cooperative: This cooperative provides training in modern farming techniques, financial literacy and business management, helping dairy farmers transition from informal to formal agricultural practices.

Rwanda Cooperative Agency: Cooperatives in Rwanda offer social protection benefits to their members, including health insurance and retirement savings, helping to formalize employment in various sectors.

Artisanal cooperatives in Tunisia offer training in business management, quality control and design. They also facilitate access for artisans to national and international markets, enhancing the visibility and sales of their products. Artisans who join these cooperatives have the opportunity to formalize their businesses, access formal contracts, and obtain social security benefits and health insurance.[75]

Women's cooperatives in Jordan provide training, access to credit, and support in product development and marketing. These cooperatives assist women in formalizing their businesses and improving their entrepreneurial skills. By joining cooperatives, women can transition from informal to formal economic activities, gaining access to financial services and social benefits.[76]

Argan oil cooperatives in Morocco offer training in sustainable harvesting and oil extraction techniques. They also aid members in marketing their products both locally and internationally, ensuring fair prices and stable incomes. Women in these cooperatives can formalize their work, gain access to social security benefits, and enhance their economic independence.[77]

Agricultural marketing cooperatives in the occupied Palestinian territory provide training, technical assistance and access to financial services. These cooperatives help farmers improve the quality of their products and access better markets, both locally and internationally. Farmers involved in these cooperatives can formalize their agricultural activities, gain access to formal credit, and secure improved incomes.[78]

7. Concluding observations and practical policy recommendations for just transitions

A. Concluding observations

Informality reflects systemic issues like governance deficiencies, unequal development and social exclusion. A holistic approach beyond reactionary policies is required. Sustainable transition to formality necessitates an integrated policy framework embedded in national development strategies with adequate funding and coordination across government agencies, labour unions and private sector actors. Governments should first conduct a comprehensive assessment of informality drivers and impacts before designing tailored, inclusive policies that consider economic, social and cultural factors.

Investing in data forecasts and utilizing models such as ARIMAX can lead to informed and well-articulated policies. ARIMAX revealed that policy inertia will deepen informality over time. The results showed the need for immediate labour market interventions and the importance of evidence-based policy designs.

Key steps include mapping vulnerabilities, collecting baseline data, and monitoring the impact of formalization on workers and communities. Transparent governance, decentralized decision-making and digital tools such as mobile platforms and e-governance portals can streamline administrative processes, ensuring broader participation. Digital inclusion, supported by affordable Internet access, is essential for bridging the gap for informal workers and businesses.

Effective outreach is critical, requiring public campaigns to promote formalization benefits, highlight success stories, and engage stakeholders. Tailored, region-specific awareness efforts, supported by non-governmental organizations, trade unions and cooperatives, can dispel misconceptions and build trust in formalization initiatives.

Ultimately, just transition to formality requires a renewed social contract that prioritizes equity, social protection and decent work for all. Governments must shift cultural perceptions by demonstrating the benefits of formalization, encouraging a gradual and inclusive transition and ensuring sustainable economic development and social equity.

B. Suggested practical solutions for Governments

Policymakers must create inclusive frameworks that balance incentives with enforcement, prioritize social justice, and integrate technology. A holistic approach combining streamlined processes, financial incentives, tax reductions, social protections and targeted interventions is key to encouraging transitioning from informality. The following policy solutions are based on successful models and should be adapted to local contexts, considering the size of the informal sector and political will.

1. Embark on regulatory and legislative reforms and enhance policy coherence

Labour law reforms must explicitly address non-standard employment relationships to ensure comprehensive protection for vulnerable populations. Global precedents, such as the integration of e-platform users into labour law frameworks, can serve as valuable models for adoption.

To facilitate effective transition from informal to formal employment, labour law reforms must focus on safeguarding the rights of all workers, particularly those situated in precarious sectors. This encompasses gig workers,[79] domestic workers, street vendors and seasonal labourers, many of whom experience barriers to accessing social security, equitable wages and essential workplace protections. Governments must modernize labour codes to accurately reflect the dynamics of the digital economy and contemporary informal employment practices.

Enhanced inter-agency collaboration among labour, finance, trade and social protection sectors improves the development of cohesive and responsive programmes. Decentralization empowers local governments to tailor strategies that address specific regional contexts.

2. Strengthen institutional mechanisms and increase compliance

Strong institutions foster an enabling environment that encourages formalization through the establishment of clear regulations, streamlined administrative processes, reduced bureaucratic obstacles, accessible social protection, and enhanced inspection and enforcement mechanisms. Strong institutions promote compliance with labour and tax legislation and restore citizen trust in these institutions.

Box 5. A suggested model for tax incentives

Innovative tools, particularly digital platforms such as single window systems, can streamline registration, taxation and policy monitoring. Such platforms reduce bureaucratic obstacles, making it easier for informal workers and micro enterprises to comply with formalization requirements. Digital solutions also enable Governments to track economic activity, assess policy effectiveness, and fine-tune interventions based on real-time data. Financial technology, mobile banking and blockchain can be used to make taxation and registration processes more accessible to informal businesses, helping them to integrate into the formal sector without creating undue financial burdens.

Taxation policies are key to formalization. The monotax model in Latin America simplifies this by merging tax and social security into a single payment. In Uruguay, it helped small and micro businesses and independent workers join the formal economy while accessing benefits including pensions and healthcare. This approach can be adapted with tiered contributions for sectors with seasonal incomes, such as agriculture, domestic work and street vending.

For gig workers, new taxation models could ensure compliance while maintaining flexibility. Automatic tax withholding by digital platforms, direct remittance to tax authorities, or integrated tax accounts would facilitate compliance for platform-based workers, reducing administrative burdens. Presumptive taxation, which estimates tax liability based on observable business indicators such as electricity usage, workforce size or estimated turnover, could simplify taxation for small businesses and micro enterprises, minimizing the need for complex bookkeeping.

Tax incentive programmes are another key tool in promoting formalization. Governments can offer tax holidays to newly formalized businesses, gradually phasing in obligations to ease the transition. Compliance rewards, such as linking tax payments to access to credit, government contracts or subsidies, can further encourage informal businesses to register. Flexible tax models, such as sector-specific taxation, including fixed monthly contributions or income-based taxes, can be adapted to seasonal work patterns, allowing businesses to pause contributions during economic downturns.

Hybrid tax-social protection systems offer additional incentives by directly linking tax compliance to social benefits. Providing tax credits to informal businesses that register workers for social security schemes or requiring employers to contribute to portable accounts funding health insurance, pensions or unemployment benefits, could create a more secure and attractive formalization pathway. Such schemes would also ensure that workers transitioning to formality experience tangible improvements in social protection.

With the growth of gig platforms and digital transactions, real-time tax collection via financial technology and blockchain can enhance transparency, reduce evasion, and ensure fair contributions. However, safeguards are needed to prevent large corporations from exploiting systems designed for small businesses. Strengthening inspections, legal enforcement and cross-agency collaboration is key.

Formalization costs vary. While some sectors benefit from integration, others may need alternative support or protection measures rather than strict formalization mandates.

3. Simplify registration processes and leverage the use of technology solutions

Streamlining administrative and registration procedures is critical for lowering barriers informal workers and businesses seeking to enter the formal economy face. User-friendly processes should capitalize on existing networks, such as post offices and banks, as registration hubs, and should be supplemented by technology-friendly and mobile-friendly platforms to facilitate the digitization of registration, tax declarations and payment processes. Simplified and decentralized services can improve accessibility, particularly in rural and peri-urban areas.

4. Provide financial incentives and tailored reductions in taxes

Implementing targeted financial incentives, such as subsidies, microfinance programmes, affordable credit, tax holidays and a fair taxation system, can mobilize resources for formalization initiatives. Low and capped tax rates, such as the fixed rates of 1 per cent-2 per cent in Morocco, make formalization financially viable, while graduated or tiered taxation ensures that micro and small businesses are not overwhelmed as they grow. Subsidizing initial costs for first-time registrants and providing targeted support such as collateral-free loans and credit facilities can further alleviate financial burdens. Programmes like the Auto-Entrepreneur in Morocco have successfully created pathways for micro enterprises to formalize, and examples such as the Mudra loans in India and MSME programmes in Nigeria show the potential of tailored financial support in promoting formalization across diverse sectors.

5. Expand social protection coverage

Extending affordable and flexible social protection systems, including health insurance, pensions and maternity benefits, can incentivize informal workers to formalize. Schemes must be customized to address the specific needs of marginalized groups, such as women, young people and older persons. For instance, to provide financial security and accommodate the income volatility of informal workers, Governments can introduce flexible contributory and non-contributory plans that allow workers to make subsidized or nominal payments at irregular intervals. Offering subsidized or free health insurance coverage to informal workers, ensuring access to essential medical services, would serve as a significant incentive. In rural areas, community health insurance schemes can be particularly effective.

By implementing cooperative models, portable benefits and crisis-responsive schemes, Governments can enhance the attractiveness and accessibility of formalization. Cooperative-based models such as the Sociétés Mutuelles de Services Agricoles in Tunisia, and portable benefits such as in Argentina and India, can improve accessibility and facilitate transitions across sectors. Emergency support, including cash transfers and subsidies during crises, further safeguards workers against a relapse into informality. The mandated social security coverage for all workers in Tunisia provides an example.

6. Establish a national task force to enhance coordination

Establishing a national task force comprised of all relevant government agencies dedicated to facilitating the transition to a formal economy can enhance tax compliance, expand the revenue base, promote social protection, improve awareness and outreach, and contribute to sustainable economic development. The task force would play a crucial role in ensuring a structured, inclusive and sustainable transition. Its primary function will be to serve as a coordination and communication mechanism that promotes dialogue among key stakeholders, ensures inclusivity in decision-making, prevents duplication of efforts, and streamlines resources and initiatives. The task force can ensure the development and implementation of a cross-government coordinated strategy while enhancing coordination in data collection and sharing. In collaboration with national authorities and ministries, the task force can act as the custodian of electronic records and maintain up-to-date data to better inform policymaking.

7. Promote collective structures such as social solidarity economy

The social solidarity economy emphasizes equitable, community-driven solutions, providing a gender-sensitive lens to address the care economy and unpaid work. Cooperative models and participatory frameworks can transform informal networks into structured, sustainable entities. Encouraging the formation of cooperatives and social solidarity enterprises enables informal workers to pool resources, access credit, and formalize their activities.

Supportive legal frameworks are critical to ensuring the success of these collective models. Farmer-producer organizations, such as those promoted in India, illustrate how cooperatives can integrate small-scale producers into formal value chains, fostering economic resilience and sustainability.

8. Develop targeted policy interventions and scale up successful pilot projects

Equitable access to formalization programmes requires targeted policies that address regional disparities and prioritize sectors characterized by high levels of informality. Sector-specific and demographic-focused interventions must address the unique challenges faced by high-informality sectors and vulnerable populations. Gradual formalization schemes and phased policy sequencing should accommodate the realities of informal workers and enterprises. By aligning incentives with local socioeconomic conditions, Governments can build trust and foster voluntary compliance.

Policies tailored to agriculture, handicrafts and domestic work, alongside initiatives focused on women and young people, such as entrepreneurship training, financial support and seed funding, can facilitate formalization efforts. Safety nets and targeted incentives for older workers transitioning to formal employment further enhance inclusivity. Decentralized services and mobile teams can address gaps in rural and underserved areas. Customized support for rural women entrepreneurs, such as in Jordan, Morocco and Tunisia, as well as interventions in agriculture, domestic work and construction, can integrate marginalized workers into formal systems, promoting broader socioeconomic inclusion. Successful pilot projects should be scaled to national levels, accompanied by increased funding and strategic efforts for expansion. Initiatives such as the Sociétés Mutuelles de Services Agricoles in Tunisia and rural programmes in Morocco illustrate the viability of implementing tested models on a larger scale.

9. Foster entrepreneurship by upskilling and business development services

Education and vocational training tailored to market demands enhances worker employability and improves enterprise productivity. Empowering informal workers through entrepreneurship is crucial for achieving sustainable formalization. Establishing incubators and business advisory services can support emerging entrepreneurs, while the integration of digital tools and technologies can enhance operational efficiency. Innovative training programmes focused on green jobs and sustainable practices can align formalization efforts with broader development objectives.

Business development services should be promoted to improve financial literacy, business management, licensing and registration, and marketing to equip workers with essential skills. Mentorship initiatives can connect them with experienced entrepreneurs for guidance, offer market access and integration into value chains and provide access to credit and finance. Youth-focused programmes, such as Forsa in Morocco, encourage innovation and provide seed funding, fostering a culture of entrepreneurship that bridges the informal and formal sectors.

10. Address long-term structural education and gender disparity issues

The Arab region's educated young people turn to informality due to restricted labour market entry, skills mismatch, and the lack of education-employment linkages. Governments in the region should invest in the mid- to long-term overhaul of education systems to align curricula with labour market needs, expand vocational training, and foster university-industry partnerships. Governments need to do more to encourage private sector growth and investment in sectors with high formal employment potential, along with enhancing job-matching services and providing incentives for formal hiring. Implementing policies that promote women's formal employment such as childcare support, equal pay regulations and non-discriminatory hiring practices is also key to addressing gender disparities.

Annex. Evolution of the International Conference of Labour Statisticians Standards

Figure A.1 Major milestones of ICLS resolutions on standards for measuring informality

15th ICLS (1993)

Defined the informal sector for statistical purposes, based on the characteristics of production units, particularly focusing on unincorporated enterprises owned by households that are not registered or regulated. Distinguished between the formal and informal sectors based on legal frameworks, scale and registration. Identified informal employment by focusing on characteristics of enterprises.

17th ICLS (2003)

Broadened focus from informal sector to informal employment (formal and informal sectors).
Identified four categories of informal employment: (a) own-account workers and employers in informal enterprises; (b) contributing family workers; (c) employees holding informal jobs without social protection or formal contracts; and (d) members of informal producer cooperatives.

19th ICLS (2013)

Consolidated previous resolutions and addressed overlaps in defining informal employment.
Maintained emphasis on the enterprise-based approach (5th ICLS) which focused on employment in the informal sector but also adopted the worker-focused approach (17th ICLS) focusing on informal employment.
Broadened understanding by introducing new concept of informal productive activities and five forms of work (own-use production, employment, unpaid trainee, volunteer work, and other forms of work such as unpaid family work).

ILO Recom. No. 204 (2015)

Considered the first international labour standard focusing on the informal economy in all its forms and calling for transitioning to the formal economy.
Provided guidance on the process of formalization.

21st ICLS (2023)

Reflected complexities, established new criteria for assessing various employment types, and acknowledged new modalities.
Recognized standard employment forms like full-time, stable positions with consistent hours, remuneration and social protections; and non-standard employment such as part-time, temporary or gig work.

Source: Developed by the authors based on information obtained from ICLS resolutions of 1993, 2003, 2013, 2023 and ILO recommendation (No. 204).

The 15th ICLS resolution (1993) established a statistical definition of the informal sector, distinguishing it based on the characteristics of production units, particularly unincorporated, unregistered and unregulated household enterprises. This definition helped differentiate formal and informal sectors using legal frameworks, scale and registration, emphasizing an enterprise-based approach to identifying informal employment.[80]

In 2002, the ILO expanded the definition of the informal economy to include both informal employment and production relationships, covering informal jobs within formal enterprises. It defined the informal economy as all economic activities by workers and units not covered or insufficiently covered by formal arrangements. These activities may operate outside legal frameworks, lack enforcement, or face compliance barriers due to burdensome regulations or high costs.[81]

In 2003, the 17th ICLS expanded the focus from the informal sector to informal employment across both formal and informal sectors. It defined informal employment as jobs lacking legal or social protection, regardless of the sector. The resolution shifted the emphasis from enterprises to workers and employment relationships, identifying four main categories: own-account workers and employers in informal enterprises, contributing family workers, employees without social protection or formal contracts, and members of informal producer cooperatives.[82]

The 19th ICLS (2013) consolidated previous resolutions by integrating both enterprise-based (15th ICLS) and worker-focused (17th ICLS) approaches to defining informal employment. It introduced the concept of informal productive activities, expanding the scope beyond employment in informal enterprises to include unregulated work such as subsistence farming, unpaid family work, casual labour and paid domestic work outside formal systems. It broadened labour statistics by defining five forms of work: own-use production, employment, unpaid trainee work, volunteer work and other unpaid labour, recognizing that informal activities can exist even within formal jobs.[83]

In 2015, ILO adopted Recommendation No. 204, the first international labour standard addressing the informal economy and advocating for its transition to formality.[84] The 2030 Agenda for Sustainable Development reinforced this goal through Sustainable Development Goal 8, particularly target 8.3, which promotes policies supporting productive employment, entrepreneurship and the formalization of MSMEs. These two frameworks are key milestones guiding global efforts towards formalization.

The 21st ICLS (2023) refined labour market principles to reflect modern employment complexities. It introduced new criteria for assessing employment types, distinguishing between standard employment (full-time, stable jobs with social protections), non-standard employment (part-time, temporary, gig work), and dependent contractors (legally independent but economically reliant on a single employer). The resolution emphasized the need for comprehensive labour statistics on job quality, employment relationships and workers' access to social assistance.[85]

Endnotes

1. Prindex, 2024.
2. International Labour Organization (ILO), n.d. Note: Statistics are based on latest available year.
3. Ibid. Note: Statistics are based on latest available year.
4. Ibid. Note: Statistics are based on ILO estimates for 2024.
5. United Nations Economic and Social Commission for Western Asia (ESCWA), 2021. Note: This number does not take into account COVID-19 repercussions or that over 85 per cent of young people in the region are informally employed without job security and social protection.
6. ILO, 2024.
7. ESCWA, 2023.
8. ILO. 2020.
9. Asia Development Dialogue, 2015.
10. ILO, 2023a.
11. ILO, 2023b.
12. ILO, 2023c.
13. Ibid.
14. The gig economy refers to labour markets characterized by short-term contracts or freelance work as opposed to permanent jobs. It includes work mediated through digital labour platforms as well as other forms of independent contracting, where workers are paid for individual tasks or projects rather than receiving a regular wage or salary. Source: ILO, 2021b.
15. ILO, 2023b.
16. The regional average for informal employment is based on available data in 12 Arab countries.
17. Regional average is based on 12 Arab countries for which data is available spanning over a period from 2014-2024. ESCWA calculations based on ILOSTAT, latest available year by country.
18. ESCWA calculations based on ILOSTAT, latest available year by country. Based on 12 Arab countries.
19. ILO, 2023c.
20. ESCWA calculations based on Informal Enterprises Survey.
21. World Bank Group, 2016.
22. Labour informality in Uruguay fell 17 points in the last decade, according to an ECLAC study, available at https://www.cepal.org/en/noticias/la-informalidad-uruguay-cayo-17-puntos-la-ultima-decada-destaca-estudio-cepal.
23. Arab Region consists of the 22 Arab countries namely: Algeria, Bahrain, Comoros, Djibouti, Egypt, Iraq, Jordan, Kuwait, Lebanon, Libya, Morocco, Mauritania, Oman, Palestine, Qatar, Saudi Arabia, Sudan, Somalia, Syrian Arab Republic, Tunisia, United Arab Emirates, Yemen.
24. ILO, 2023d.
25. ESCWA, 2022.
26. World Bank Group, 2022b.
27. ILO, 2021a.
28. Ibid.

29. World Bank Group, 2014.
30. Ibid.
31. PwC, 2019.
32. Andersen, 2021.
33. PwC, 2019.
34. Organisation for Economic Co-operation and Development (OECD), 2020.
35. ILO, 2016.
36. Sankaran, 2022.
37. WIEGO, 2013.
38. ESCWA calculations based on Informal Sector Enterprise Surveys of Iraq, Somalia and the Sudan.
39. OECD and ILO, 2019.
40. The International Standard Industrial Classification of All Economic Activities (ISIC) is the international reference classification of productive activities. Its main purpose is to provide a set of activity categories that can be utilized for the collection and reporting of statistics according to such activities.
41. Government of Jordan, 2022.
42. United Nations Trade and Development (UNCTAD), 2017.
43. OECD, ILO and UNDP, 2024.
44. World Bank Group, n.d.
45. OECD, 2021.
46. ILO, 2021a.
47. OECD, ILO and UNDP, 2024.
48. ILO, 2016.
49. OECD, 2024.
50. OECD, ILO and UNDP, 2024.
51. World Bank Group, 2023.
52. World Bank Group, 2022a.
53. Global Development Research Center, n.d.
54. ARIMAX: Autoregressive Integrated Moving Average with Exogenous Variables.
55. Baqua, 2023.
56. Kingdom of Morocco – Ministry of Industry and Trade, n.d.
57. Mouelhi, Ben Braham and Ghazali, 2021.
58. Belhaj Rhouma and Ahmed, 2018.
59. Folawewo and Orija, 2020.
60. Okeagu, 2022.
61. PwC, n.d.
62. Abramo, 2022.
63. Ibid.
64. Ibid.
65. Natarajan, Schotte and Sen, 2020.
66. Ibid.
67. Ibid.

68. Sopheavotey, 2024.

69. PPCBank, 2022.

70. Partech, 2020.

71. Bombarda and Lopes, 2021.

72. BATS – Strategy Research Consulting, n.d.

73. NATLEX ILO, n.d.

74. Ghonem, 2019.

75. Government of Tunisia – Ministry of Woman, Family and Childhood, 2017.

76. Tamkeen and others, 2025.

77. Reuters, 2021.

78. International Cooperative Alliance Asia and the Pacific, 2022.

79. Gig workers are individuals who earn income through short-term, task- or project-based work outside traditional, long-term employer–employee relationships—often (but not exclusively) matched via online/digital platforms. They are typically paid per task/assignment and engaged as independent contractors or other non-standard arrangements, rather than open-ended employees. Source: OECD, Competition in Labour Markets, 2020.

80. ILO, 1993.

81. ILO, 2002.

82. ILO, 2003.

83. ILO, 2013.

84. ILO, 2015.

85. ILO, 2023b.

Bibliography

Abramo, Laís (2022). Policies to address the challenges of existing and new forms of informality in Latin America. Social Policy series, No. 240 (LC/TS.2021/137), Santiago, Economic Commission for Latin America and the Caribbean (ECLAC).

Andersen (2021). Non-Cash Payment Law No. 18 of 2019.

Asia Development Dialogue (2015). Extending Livelihood Opportunities and Social Protection to Empower Poor Urban Informal Workers in Asia. WIEGO.

Baqua, Chaimaa (2023). Adherence to auto-entrepreneur status drops by 34 per cent in Morocco after years of popularity. HESPRESS English – Morocco News. Available at https://en.hespress.com/69086-adherence-to-auto-entrepreneur-status-drops-by-34-in-morocco-after-years-of-popularity.html.

BATS – Strategy Research Consulting (n.d.). Payroll Peru. Available at https://bats-consulting.com/payroll/1ff8a7b5dc7a7d1f0ed65aaa29c04b1e.

Belhaj Rhouma, Akram and Zied Ahmed (2018). Les sociétés mutuelles de services agricoles (SMSA) en Tunisie: cadre juridique et partenariat Public-SMSA. CIHEAM-IAMM.

Bombarda, Luisa, and Layon Lopes (2021). Simples Nacional: What do you need to know. Available at https://silvalopes.adv.br/simples-nacional-what-do-you-need-to-know.

Folawewo, Abiodun O. and Olusegun A. Orija (2020). Informal–formal workers' transition in Nigeria: A livelihood analysis. WIDER Working Paper 2020/146.

Ghonem, Magda (2019). Egypt: Review of the agrifood cooperative sector. Country highlights FAO Investment Centre. Food and Agriculture Organization of the United Nations.

Global Development Research Center (n.d.). Exploring the Informal Sector: Five Key Inquiries and Insights. Available at https://www.gdrc.org/informal/5-questions.html.

Government of Jordan (2022). Reform matrix: 2021 at a glance.

Government of Tunisia – Ministry of Woman, Family and Childhood (2017). National Strategy for the Economic and Social Empowerment of Women and Girls in Rural Areas 2017-2020. Available at https://nwm.unescwa.org/resources/326.

International Cooperative Alliance Asia and the Pacific (2022). Cooperatives in the State of Palestine. Available at https://icaap.coop/wp-content/uploads/2024/05/20March22_Palestine-Country-Snapshot.pdf.

International Labour Organization (n.d.). Labour Force Statistics database ILOSTAT. Available at ilostat.ilo.org/data. Accessed on 15 October 2024.

__________ (1993). Fifteenth International Conference of Labour Statisticians - General Report. Available at https://webapps.ilo.org/public/libdoc/ilo/1992/92B09_219_engl.pdf.

__________ (2002). Resolution and conclusions concerning decent work and the informal economy. International Labour Conference, 90th Session, para. 6, as reproduced in Appendix I.

__________ (2003). Seventeenth International Conference of Labour Statisticians - Guidelines concerning a statistical definition of informal employment. Available at https://www.ilo.org/sites/default/files/wcmsp5/groups/public/@dgreports/@stat/documents/normativeinstrument/wcms_087622.pdf.

__________ (2013). Nineteenth International Conference of Labour Statisticians - Report of the Conference. (2013). Available at https://www.ilo.org/sites/default/files/wcmsp5/groups/public/@dgreports/@stat/documents/publication/wcms_234124.pdf.

__________ (2015). International Labour Conference - Recommendation No. 204 concerning the transition from the informal to the formal economy. Available at https://www.ilo.org/resource/ilc/104/recommendation-no-204-concerning-transition-informal-formal-economy.

__________ (2016). Policies, Strategies and Practices for the Formalisation of Micro and Small Enterprises.

__________ (2020). Impact of lockdown measures on the informal economy: A summary.

__________ (2021a). Identifying barriers to formalization: A snapshot of key challenges in South Africa's informal economy, including in times of Covid-19, and suggested measures on how to get policies and incentive structures right.

_________ (2021b). World Employment and Social Outlook: The Role of Digital Labour Platforms in Transforming the World of Work.

_________ (2023a). New standards, increased visibility: improving measurement of the informal economy. ILOSTAT. Available at https://ilostat.ilo.org/blog/new-standards-increased-visibility-improving-measurement-of-the-informal-economy/.

_________ (2023b). Twenty-First International Conference of Labour Statisticians: Report of the Conference. Available at https://www.ilo.org/sites/default/files/wcmsp5/groups/public/@dgreports/@stat/documents/meetingdocument/wcms_908954.pdf.

_________ (2023c). Women and men in the informal economy: A statistical update.

_________ (2023d). World Employment and Social Outlook – Trends 2023.

_________ (2024). Global Employment Trends for Youth 2024 Decent work, brighter futures.

Kingdom of Morocco – Ministry of Industry and Trade (n.d.). Self-employed status: a true success and results exceeding expectations. Available at https://www.mcinet.gov.ma/en/content/self-employed-status-true-success-and-results-exceeding-expectations. Accessed on 7 January 2025.

Mouelhi, Rim Ben Ayed, Mehdi Ben Braham and Monia Ghazali (2021). The social and solidarity economy in Tunisia and its role in formalising the informal economy: a qualitative survey. EU-Mediterranean and African Network for Economic Studies (EMNES), Working Paper No 48.

Natarajan, Rajesh Raj, Simone Schotte, and Kunal Sen (2020). Transitions between informal and formal jobs in India: Patterns, correlates, and consequences. WIDER Working Paper 2020/101.

NATLEX ILO (n.d.). LXXV of 2010 law on simplified employment. Available at https://natlex.ilo.org/dyn/natlex2/natlex2/files/download/105203/HUN-105203.pdf.

Okeagu, Joy (2022). Formalization of business enterprises in Nigeria: a review of Nigeria's policies on micro, small and medium enterprises. University of Edinburgh.

Organisation for Economic Co-operation and Development (2020). OECD Investment Policy Reviews: Egypt 2020. Available at https://doi.org/10.1787/9f9c589a-en.

_________ (2021). Informality and COVID-19 in Eurasia: The Sudden Loss of a Social Buffer.

_________ (2024). OECD Economic Surveys: Egypt 2024. Available at https://www.oecd.org/en/publications/oecd-economic-surveys-egypt-2024_af900de2-en.html.

Organisation for Economic Co-operation and Development and International Labour Organization (2019). Tackling Vulnerability in the Informal Economy. Development Centre Studies. Available at https://doi.org/10.1787/939b7bcd-en.

Organisation for Economic Co-operation and Development, International Labour Organization and United Nations Development Programme (2024). Informality and Structural Transformation in Egypt, Iraq and Jordan.

Partech (2020). TradeDepot secures additional $10M to transform the informal retail supply chain in Nigeria. Available at https://partechpartners.com/news/tradedepot-secures-additional-10m-transform-informal-retail-supply-chain-nigeria.

PPCBank (2022). Pay National Social Security Fund (NSSF) Contributions with PPCBank Free of Charge! Available at https://www.ppcbank.com.kh/pay-national-social-security-fund-nssf-contributions-with-ppcbank-free-of-charge.

Prindex (2024). Data on tenure insecurity by age Available at https://prindex.net/.

PwC (n.d.). Corporate – tax credits and incentives: Ghana. Available at https://taxsummaries.pwc.com/ghana/corporate/tax-credits-and-incentives.

_________ (2019). Shedding light on Egypt's shadow economy.

Reuters (2021). Meet the Moroccan women making Argan oil for the beauty industry. Available at https://www.reuters.com/world/meet-moroccan-women-making-argan-oil-beauty-industry-2021-06-15/.

Sankaran, Kamala (2022). Transition from the Informal to the Formal Economy: The Need for a Multi-faceted Approach. The Indian Journal of Labour Economics. 65:625–642. Available at https://doi.org/10.1007/s41027-022-00398-2.

Sopheavotey, Lay (2024). PM clarifies: digital platform for informal worker support, not taxation. CamNess. Available at https://cambodianess.com/article/pm-clarifies-digital-platform-for-informal-worker-support-not-taxation.

Tamkeen and others (2025). Cooperatives and their role in supporting the Jordanian agricultural sector. Available at https://tamkeen-jo.org/sites/default/files/2025-03/Cooperatives%20and%20Their%20Role%20in%20Supporting%20the%20Jordanian%20Agricultural%20Sector.pdf.

United Nations Economic and Social Commission for Western Asia (2021). Towards a Productive and Inclusive Path Job Creation in the Arab Region.

Available at https://www.unescwa.org/publications/productive-inclusive-path-job-creation-arab-region.

_________ (2022). Survey of Economic and Social Developments in the Arab Region 2021–2022.

_________ (2023). Survey of Economic and Social Developments in the Arab Region 2022-2023. Available at https://www.unescwa.org/sites/default/files/pubs/pdf/survey-economic-social-developments-arab-region-2022-2023-english_0.pdf.

United Nations Trade and Development (UNCTAD) (2017). Executive Regulations for Industrial Permits Act issued. Available at https://investmentpolicy.unctad.org/investment-policy-monitor/measures/3143/egypt-executive-regulations-for-industrial-permits-act-issued-#:~:text=The per cent20executive per cent20regulations per cent20bring per cent20into,order per cent20to per cent20secure per cent20a per cent20licence.

WIEGO (2013). Formalizing Street vendors. Available at https://www.wiego.org/advocacy-worker-education-resources/formalizing-street-vendors-presentation-dialogue-formalization-informal/.

World Bank Group (n.d.). Doing Business Data. Available at https://archive.doingbusiness.org/en/data.

_________ (2014). Informal Firms and Financial Inclusion: Status and Determinants.

_________ (2016). Retaking the path to inclusion, growth and sustainability: Brazil systematic country diagnostic.

_________ (2022a). Informal Sector Enterprise Surveys: What Businesses Experience. Profile of Cities in Sudan 2022.

_________ (2022b). Jobs Undone: Reshaping the Role of Governments Toward Active Labor Market Policies in MENA.

_________ (2023). Understanding Urban Informality in Iraq: Findings from the Informal Sector Enterprise Survey.